Stadium Stories:
Dallas Cowboys

D1565252

Stadium Stories™ Series

Stadium Stories:

Dallas Cowboys

Colorful Tales of America's Team

Brad Sham

The Globe Pequot Press

GUILFORD, CONNECTICUT

Copyright © 2003 by The Globe Pequot Press

Stadium Stories is a trademark of The Globe Pequot Press.

Text design: Casey Shain
All photos courtesy *Dallas Cowboys Weekly* except where noted.

Library of Congress Cataloging-in-Publication Data is available.

ISBN 0-7627-2759-4

Manufactured in the United States of America
First Edition/First Printing

For Mom and Dad

Contents

Acknowledgments

The author wishes to thank the people without whose help this book would just be a collection of random thoughts: my wife, Peggy, for all her help and support; from Globe Pequot Press, editors Mike Urban and Mary Norris; my attorneys, Paul Schoonover and Jamey Newberg; from the *Dallas Cowboys Weekly*, Russ Russell and Cheryl Harris; from the National Football League, Vince Casey; from the U.S. Naval Academy, sports information director Scott Strasemeier; from the *Dallas Morning News*, Frank Luksa; from Cowboys teams past and present, Tex Schramm, Jerry Jones, Troy Aikman, Joe Avezzano, Larry Cole, Jason Garrett, Cliff Harris, Chad Hennings, Michael Irvin, Daryl Johnston, Larry Lacewell, Babe Laufenberg, Bob Lilly, Blaine Nye, Bill Parcells, Drew Pearson, Preston Pearson, Emmitt Smith, Gene Stallings, Roger Staubach, Pat Toomay, Charlie Waters, Danny White, and Darren Woodson; and from the Dallas Cowboys public relations department, great and good friends Rich Dalrymple and Brett Daniels, who will be thrilled to learn I have no more questions relating to this project.

Twenty-Five Years in the Booth

Autumn 1976. The Oakland Raiders were on their way to beating Minnesota in the Super Bowl under Coach John Madden. The Cincinnati Reds were on their way to a four-game sweep of the New York Yankees for the Big Red Machine's second straight World Series title. Jimmy Carter was on his way to defeating incumbent Gerald Ford to win the presidency of the United States.

It was my first autumn in the Dallas Cowboys' radio broadcast booth.

The 2003 season marks my twenty-fifth broadcasting Cowboys games. (I know, the math doesn't compute. There was a three-year hiatus to broadcast Texas Rangers baseball from 1995–97.) That's 364 regular-season games, thirty play-offs, and ninety-two in the preseason. I've been involved in broadcasting 486 Dallas Cowboys games. No wonder I'm tired.

It's been a wild ride. I've had the privilege of working four Super Bowls and the agony of trying to describe pleasantly a 1–15 season. I've found myself interviewing not just football players and executives, but also Howard Cosell and Prince Bandar of Saudi Arabia. I've sat idle while games were canceled because of one players' strike and worked when replacement players were hired during another.

And I missed one game. In the strike season of 1982, a makeup game was added at the end of the season. The Cowboys were in Bloomington, Minnesota, to end the regular year with a Monday night game against the Vikings at old Metropolitan Stadium.

As they do now, the Cowboys hosted a hospitality suite in their hotel. The night before the game, the suite was opened for reporters and photographers to join club guests and staff, and in those days assistant coaches, for snacks and lively conversation and beverages. The beverages were frequently the focal point. As was my custom, I focused on the snacks.

It might have been a faulty onion dip or some rumaki gone bad. But on Monday morning, January 3, 1983, I awoke, to be delicate, not of my own accord. And considerably the worse for wear.

When I could make it to the telephone, I dialed our flagship station, at that time KRLD in Dallas, and told operations manager Gary Brandt I had doubts about my availability for that night. In those days I was the color analyst for play-by-play announcer Verne Lundquist, and I told Brandt he should call Charlie Waters and get him on a plane. Waters, the Cowboys former all-pro safety, had done some stellar broadcast work with us in the past, and he was finishing his first year of retirement.

It turned out to be the correct move. I was, uh, confined to my room for the day. Being in Minnesota, though, I couldn't pick up our radio broadcast of the game. So I had to watch the Cowboys end the season with a 31–27 loss on television.

And therefore I couldn't hear Verne and Charlie describe one of the greatest single moments in Cowboys' history: Tony Dorsett's 99-yard touchdown run with ten men on the field.

I eat fewer hospitality room snacks these days. And I've learned my lesson about what you miss when you miss a game.

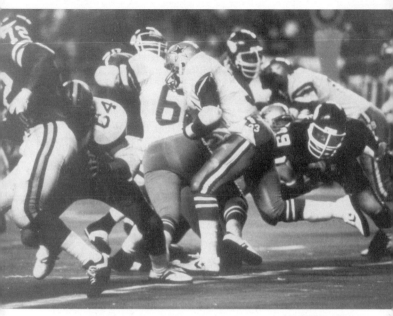

Tony Dorsett gets started on his record 99-yard run against the Vikings in January 1983.

Twenty-five years broadcasting games for "America's Team" would be a fortunate streak for anyone. As for me, I had a few reasons early on to doubt it would last that long.

When I joined KRLD in October 1976, there were two acknowledged "Voices of the Cowboys": my new partner, Verne Lundquist, who actually called most of the games, and the late Frank Glieber, who was a full-time announcer with CBS-TV. Among his myriad assignments Frank did NFL games for the network. But he'd been in Dallas since the early days of the franchise, and he had an almost brotherly relationship with Coach Tom Landry and General Manager Tex Schramm.

On Monday nights KRLD broadcast Schramm's weekly call-in show, *Ask Tex Schramm*, and Frank was the host, a position he held until his death in 1985. The show was actually aired from a tiny, closet-size studio we had at the Cowboys' office on the eleventh floor of a Dallas office tower. One of my early jobs was to operate the control board for that show back at the main KRLD studio.

Now, as Frank Glieber used to say frequently about himself, I didn't hire on to be an engineer. The technical side of the business isn't my strong point, but I can follow directions. The control board back in 1976 looked like an overgrown airplane cockpit console—row after row of dials and buttons and slide switches. There was an input switch on the board labeled "Cowboys office." That was our studio. When you opened the slide pot, what was said in the "office" came out through the control board. So I had three jobs: play the recorded musical intro on an old one-track cartridge, open the mike pot when the master control room activated our board after commercials, and punch up the phone calls. I prided myself on knowing when to "pot down" the caller and punch the next line so that irritating "click" was never heard on the air.

After a while I also figured out when our board was inactive during commercials, I could turn it down and eavesdrop on Frank and Tex. For a twenty-seven-year-old kid who knew no one and nothing and wanted to know everything, any access to information was a gold mine. So I spied.

This one night, just a couple months into my tenure, the Cowboys were coming off a particularly upsetting loss. They were a playoff team with high expectations and played poorly on Sunday, and by Monday night Tex Schramm still had not cheered up.

Tex liked to help himself through these shows with a vodka-based drink called a bullshot. During commercials you could hear the clinking of the ice in the glass and the deep, depressed sighs of the Cowboys president and general manager. And during one commercial break, I heard a lot more than that.

Schramm uttered an obscenity or two after a prolonged pause. And he then proceeded with the most colorful day-after reviews ever heard of the play of several key and prominent Cowboys. "F___ing Staubach" was one reference to the Cowboys quarterback that particularly caught my ear.

Let me jump back just a bit to tell you one thing about that control panel that I didn't know. If you punched up the next phone call during a break—the better to have the caller ready right away when Frank summoned him or her—and you then slid the mike pot down and cued up the call, the phone caller could *also* hear everything coming through the board and from the Cowboys' office.

Which is why, when I gave Frank the cue and we came back, and he said, "Back to the phones and thanks for waiting. You're on *Ask Tex Schramm*, go ahead please," the anonymous caller responded, "Well, thanks, and Tex, I just want to tell you, I agree with every single word you just said."

Every drop of blood drained from my face and my life flashed before my eyes. My immediate thought was, "You know, I think I'm going to like it in Midland."

Tex and Frank's conversation had not made the air, but it took me a few seconds to figure that out. When I realized what had happened, I was terrified. The only thing that saved me was that Frank knew less about how that board ran than I did. He and Tex were both puzzled, but they bluffed their way through it and went on.

I told Tex that story years later. He didn't remember it, and I can't recall if I was relieved or annoyed. I never had the courage to tell Frank. And that was another mistake I only made once.

Just a year and a half later, I thought the end had come again.

In 1977 the Cowboys won the Super Bowl, beating Denver in New Orleans. When they assembled for training camp in Thousand Oaks, California, the next summer, their kicker, Efren Herrera, decided he wanted more money, so he held out.

I was on pretty good terms with all the players, so I was flattered but not really surprised one night when Herrera called me in my training camp dorm room. He was calling to tell me he was coming into camp the next day but not to report to the team. He wanted to hold a news conference, and would I please tell all my reporter buddies?

Did I say I was flattered? Heck, I was all puffed up. He could have called any of the more prominent newspaper or television reporters, but he called me. I must be a big shot!

The Cowboys didn't take kindly to holdout players. I told Herrera that I thought he was making a mistake and he ought to just come to camp, but he was adamant. Would I spread the word or not? I said I would. Another mistake I only made once.

The first thing I did, though, was to tell club officials. I contacted scout John Wooten, a former All-Pro player in his days in the league, and also a former agent. I told him the whole story, and then I started looking for other front-office personnel. This being nighttime, most of them were out to dinner, but I found George Heddleston, the assistant public relations director, and brought him up to speed. Then I told as many reporters as I could find, and I didn't think any more of it.

At least I didn't until the next afternoon. Among my duties I was host of a nightly call-in program, *Sports Central: Dallas*. It aired at 6:00 P.M., which was 4:00 P.M. Pacific time, so I had to miss the afternoon practice. As soon as my show ended that day, I got a call from KRLD's general manager, Carl Brazell.

"Have you seen Tex today?" he asked. I had not. "Well, you might want to find him. He called me about your Herrera deal, and he's a little upset. I think it'll be okay, but you ought to work it out."

I was taken aback. I'd acted in good faith and above board, and Tex Schramm was the most powerful man in the NFL. I'd been around doing color on his radio broadcasts a year and a

I've enjoyed every minute of my twenty-five seasons in the Cowboys radio booth. (Bob Thomas)

half. This didn't sound like a fight I needed any part of. So when Schramm marched back into his dorm lobby after practice, I was waiting for him.

"Hey, Tex," I said breezily, "Got a minute?"

"Sure," he barked, but then Tex was always barking. Okay, I thought, this will be fine. We'll get it all cleared up.

I followed Schramm into his dorm suite. He closed the door. "So," I said cheerily, "I understand we've got a little mix-up to straighten out."

That's when the nuclear explosion went off.

I can't recall every word, because I was too terrified and startled. But the gist of it was that by talking to Herrera and helping him call a press conference, I was acting as his agent, I had crossed the line, and I was on the verge of being sent packing.

It turned out none of the team employees I'd told about my first call from Herrera had informed Tex that I'd done that. It might not have mattered, but trying to explain that to him was futile. Tex Schramm was in full-throated battle rage, and when he got like that, you just had to figure out how quickly and painfully you wanted to die.

But I wasn't smart enough to know that. I was 29 years old, exceedingly full of myself, and convinced I was right and he was wrong. I had the moral high ground, and by heavens I intended to hold it!

Let me interject here with a question: Have you ever been involved in a conversation during which you have an almost out-of-body experience? One where you almost literally levitate outside yourself, look down on yourself having the conversation, and want to say to yourself, "Hey, blockhead! Are you nuts? Have you lost every shred of what used to be your mind? Don't do that. Don't say that! And for sure don't say *that*!"

That was me. Here's Tex Schramm, nose to my nose, bellowing like an enraged bull moose, "You've overstepped your bounds in this camp!" And me, bellowing back, "I'm not sure it's up to you to tell me what my bounds are!" (What am I thinking? It's *his* camp, for crying out loud. He can tell me any bloody thing he likes!)

And Tex: "You're acting like you're working for him!"

And me: "I'm not working for him, and I'm not working for you!" Which technically I wasn't. I was under contract to the radio station. But with the right of refusal clause the club always had on announcers, I might have been splitting hairs just a little, don't you think?

Somehow, it ended after a few minutes that seemed like hours. I was not sent packing. What Verne Lundquist told me later was that everyone who dealt with Tex had at least one of those confrontations sooner or later. I could have used some advance notice. What I also found out was that like a lot of hot-tempered people, once Tex blew, that was it. It was over, and he didn't carry a grudge, not over something like this. There were a couple of scouts and personnel types who literally crossed the street when they saw me coming for about a week, but after a while the whole thing was forgotten.

Oh, and by the way, the Cowboys released Efren Herrera, and Rafael Septien became their kicker in 1978.

I've been more than fortunate in my dealings with players, coaches, and front office folks in twenty-five years. I don't think there are five I could name that I haven't gotten along with. But sometimes, someone takes you by surprise.

In the summer of 1983, as they usually did, the Cowboys brought to camp around a hundred rookie free agents. There was no roster limit in those days, and the Cowboys usually brought in more free agents than anyone else. That was how

Versatile Voices

they found some of their greatest players, like Drew Pearson and Cliff Harris. They were always willing to take a chance on volume. In 1983 one of their nameless, faceless free agent horde was a defensive tackle from the University of Hawaii, Mark Tuinei.

In 1982 Dallas's starting defensive line consisted of a group of all stars: Ed "Too Tall" Jones, John Dutton, Randy White, and Harvey Martin. Tuinei looked like camp fodder. But somehow he kept hanging around and hanging around, and he made the team. So did an undersized safety from Tennessee named Bill Bates. They both stuck around for wonderful careers for fifteen years.

In the mid 1980s the Cowboys needed depth in the offensive line, and they moved Tuinei to offense. They thought he had great feet and might someday make a center. By 1986 Tooey, who may have been the toughest man on the team, had become the starting left tackle. In one game in Denver, All-Pro defensive tackle Randy White was injured, and Tuinei played both ways in the line.

Tooey started on some pretty woeful teams in the late '80s, but by the time Jerry Jones and Jimmy Johnson had come in and rebuilt the Cowboys into winners, he was the anchor of a championship line. Super Bowls were won in 1992 and 1993 with Tuinei protecting quarterback Troy Aikman's blind side every play. And in December of 1994, the league noticed. Mark Tuinei, the former free agent defensive tackle, was voted to his first Pro Bowl as an offensive tackle.

By that time the Cowboys broadcasts had changed stations to KVIL-FM, and on Monday nights we aired a show from a Dallas restaurant with player guests. In late December Tuinei was one of the guests. We always gave the players gifts for being on the program—free dinners, gift certificates, that kind of thing.

The late Mark Tuinei (right) surprised the author with a plane ticket to the Pro Bowl in Honolulu in February 1995. (Courtesy Brad Sham)

This particular night, we gave Tuinei his gifts at the end of the show, and as we were signing off, he said, "Wait a minute. I've got something for you." Now, this was remarkable. Tooey and I always hit it off, and he always accepted invitations to be on our programs, but he was no publicity hound, and you usually had to get him going in an interview situation.

"Something for me?" I asked. "That's not how it works. We give to you."

"Well, I've got something for you this time," he insisted. And with what happened next, you could have knocked me over with a feather.

"You've always supported me ever since I came here and no one knew me," the gentle giant said. "You always told me I'd make the Pro Bowl some day. And I said if I did, you were coming with me. So here."

And he handed me an airplane ticket to go to the Pro Bowl in Honolulu.

You have to know professional football players to know the depth of the generosity of that gesture. But it was so like Mark Tuinei. It may have been the most touching moment of twenty-five years in the booth.

Son of a gun cost me a thousand bucks with that generosity, too. As if I were going to Hawaii without my wife.

Tex

All right, Cowboys fans, let's play a little word association. I'll give you a term, and you just say the first thing that pops into your head.

Ready?

"Dallas Cowboys."

"Tom Landry," I hear you say. Unless you're under thirty-five. Then your answer might be "Troy Aikman," "Emmitt Smith," or even "Troy, Michael (Irvin), and Emmitt."

There are no wrong answers, of course. But there is a right one.

"Tex."

Tex Schramm, who died in July 2003 at age 83, was not personally responsible for everything good or bad that's ever happened to the Dallas Cowboys. But even what he was not responsible for bears his fingerprints.

Schramm, who had been the team's president and general manager since its inception in 1960, left the employ of the Cowboys not long after Jerry Jones bought the team in February 1989. So it would be wrong to credit Schramm for the three Super Bowls Jones's teams won in 1992, 1993, and 1995.

But Jerry Jones would be the first to tell you his interest in buying the Dallas Cowboys had all to do with what the franchise became in its first thirty years. And that has everything to do with Tex Schramm.

Just as Jones recently has been the most visible symbol and spokesman of and for his team, Schramm was before him. Jones has shared the spotlight with five coaches. Schramm shared it with the only one he ever hired, Landry. He did so, most observers believe, somewhat reluctantly, but by his own design.

Sitting in the den of his Dallas home in November 2002, reviewing a career that landed him in the Pro Football Hall of Fame, Schramm recalled how his Cowboys persona developed.

"I was smart enough to know," he said, "that in my role . . . well, first, I had to *create* a role. You're never going to be a Landry. You're never going to be a [Vince] Lombardi. You're never going to be a coach who's going to be real successful. You're never going to become a [Roger] Staubach. My role was kind of a secondary role. And I tried to make it as little secondary as possible. I don't apologize for that."

And here you got the famous Schramm chuckle. It was the wise chuckle of a smart old fox who knew the value and danger of every envelope-pushing move. Or, when the move was the wrong one or one that put him in a bad light, how to take advantage of even that.

For instance, when the Cowboys went to their second consecutive Super Bowl following the 1971 season, one of their stars was running back Duane Thomas. Like many they've had through the years, Thomas was a star with baggage. He stopped talking to the media early in the season, which for a Cowboy was a high crime. No one knew the value of the media like Tex Schramm, who had come to the Cowboys as a former executive with CBS television. At Schramm's direction reporters were given the home phone numbers of every Cowboy.

So to boycott reporters was unthinkable. It was one of several of Schramm's edicts that Thomas couldn't stomach. Which is why, in a preseason news conference, Thomas said of Schramm, "He's sick, dishonest, and demented."

Schramm's response: "Two out of three isn't bad."

Although by February of 1989 the Cowboys had fallen into financial difficulty and artistic hard times (in the 1988 season they were 3–13, and they earned every yard of it), that wasn't what Jerry Jones bought. What Jones bought was what Schramm built literally from scratch, hand in hand with Landry and Gil Brandt, personnel director. Jones bought

Tex Schramm (far left) was inducted into the Hall of Fame in 1991. Also inducted (from left to right): John Hannah, Earl Campbell, Stan Jones, and Jan Stenerud.

America's Team. That may be Tex Schramm's greatest acknowledged legacy. And it wasn't his.

Let him go back to the beginning, though.

"Before I went there," he recalled, "I wanted to create something that *had* a legacy. My guideline was always the Chicago Bears, the Boston Celtics, and the New York Yankees. Something that would be really unique. It makes a difference in everyone's life that was associated with the Cowboys.

"Like the Yankees. All you've got to do is say, 'He's a former Yankee,' and that person is viewed differently. Same with the Celtics. And that's what I wanted to get for us, so that for the rest of their lives, anyone who walked into a place and people said, 'Oh, yeah, he was with the Cowboys,' that would make a difference. And I think that was accomplished."

It probably had been before the 1977 team won the organization's second Super Bowl championship. But in putting together that season's highlight reel, NFL Films, looking for a catchy title, came up with the nickname that is part of the team's heritage, even when the group on the field comes up short.

"When we were named 'America's Team,' that's when I knew we'd gotten that done," Schramm recalled. "I laughed about it. Other people didn't. But they called me and said, 'What do you think?' And I said, 'As long as it isn't attributed to me, I would be very proud.' " And here you got the chuckle again.

So even though it wasn't his idea, "America's Team" may be what you think of when you think of what Tex Schramm left the Cowboys.

But he would have loved it if you knew what else he had a hand in leaving the NFL.

The NFL of the '60s, '70s, and '80s was a very different place from the one you know today. The whole world was. And one of Schramm's motivating forces in those days was what would benefit the sport. And his eye for detail often took him beyond rules changes and league bylaws.

"By nature, I'm creative. Everything I see and do makes me think about how it should be done." This was said matter-of-factly, without bravado. "The thing is, I don't know how many of those things . . . I was responsible for or involved in [people know about]." Okay, maybe a little bravado.

How about some examples, Tex?

"Well, you know how you watch a game on television, and they take a shot from above in the blimp, and you see a field well defined by a nice, wide white sideline?"

That was yours?

"That was mine. The referee's microphone was mine. Here's another one: You know how when you watch a game, there are little arrows by the numbers of the yard line, so you can tell right away which end of the field they're at? That was my idea. I put the little flags on top of the goal posts so the kickers could see where the hell the wind was coming from. The double line markings on the 20 yard lines."

Anyone that creative is bound to have also had dozens of ideas that didn't work out so well. Since Schramm lived into his early eighties, perhaps we can forgive him not remembering too many of those details. But he lived by this credo: "If you believe in it, there are probably going to be people against it. You just have to have the confidence and determination to do it."

There may be no better example than one of the most controversial developments in the NFL in the last twenty years, another one of which Schramm was in on the developmental ground floor: instant replay.

"You're going to have instant replay in sports. Whether you want it or not, it's gonna come. I think all the sports are going there. Basketball will certainly be there. Soccer will be there. Hockey's there." As he warmed to his subject, you began to see flashes of the Tex Schramm that made him loved by his friends and reviled by his enemies, and there were plenty of both: argumentative to the point of belligerence, domineering. But always, this man loved nothing more than a good fight.

"There was a group in the league that was against instant replay, and so there was always opposition," he recalled. "It wasn't a thing where they said, 'Boy, this is going to be great, let's all go.' There was always a group that said, 'This doesn't belong in football.' This was [New York Giants owner Wellington] Mara and his general manager, George Young. 'We're against it, it's wrong.' Then, of course, wherever he went, there [you'd find] some of the [bleepers] that followed him, like Mike Brown and a group of them. [Bill] Bidwell. They were always against it."

It may be helpful here to add that Tex Schramm was one who did not suffer fools gladly. Fortunately for him, they were easy to spot. Anyone who didn't agree with him was a possibility.

"By this time," Schramm said, bringing us back to instant replay, "you didn't just need the vote we needed to pass it. Since it had become popular, you needed something like 75 percent. They were afraid of it. But they didn't kill it until I left, because I could always manage to get enough votes [to retain it]. But there are a lot of things like that that come along that can be good, if you're not afraid to make a change."

How ironic, then, that this man so unafraid of change had the last few years of his tenure as the Cowboys majordomo so sullied by his own refusal to make one. How different Tex Schramm's later years might have been had he had the stomach to dismiss Tom Landry.

Schramm and the Cowboys first owner, the late Clint Murchison, hired Landry off the New York Giants' coaching staff after the 1959 season, before the Cowboys officially had been given franchise papers. In the early 1960s, when the Cowboys struggled mightily and the fans and newspapers called for Landry's firing, Murchison told Schramm the best way to quiet the furor would be to award Landry a ten-year contract— which they did. The result was two Super Bowl championships and twenty consecutive winning seasons, among other accomplishments.

But things change. The Cowboys lost the Super Bowl after the 1978 season, then lost in the NFC Championship Game in '80, '81, and '82. Despite a 12–4 record in 1983, they finished second in the NFC East and lost a wild card playoff game to the Rams at Texas Stadium. In 1984 a streak of nine straight playoff seasons ended with a 9–7 record. The 1985 season was wildly erratic and ended with a 20–0 divisional playoff loss in Los Angeles. And in 1986 the Cowboys finished 7–9, ending a string of twenty years with a winning record.

All of which was why Landry had approached Schramm in 1985 and told him to get ready for the transition to the next coach.

"After that year," Schramm recalled, "Tom told me he was thinking about when he was going to retire and I had better start making some changes, so we could have a clean transition. So I did. That's when I started going out and looking for the best young coaches with a lot of potential." That's why, in February of 1986, Schramm hired perhaps the brightest young offensive mind in the league, Paul Hackett, from the San Francisco 49ers. (Hackett continues to draw rave reviews as an offensive coordinator into the new millennium.)

Then Landry threw Schramm a curve: In 1988 Landry told a news conference he felt up to the challenge of coaching into the '90s. (Some of us thought Tom meant his nineties.) It was the first Schramm knew of Tom's intentions.

"I had some good ones lined up. I got Wade Phillips to be the defensive coordinator. I had Marty Schottenheimer lined up to take Tom's place, after he got fired in Cleveland, but before he got hired in Kansas City," Schramm remembered. "I took Schottenheimer around looking at houses." Then, suddenly, those jobs weren't available.

"Tom gave up the idea of retiring. Here he told me to get everything lined up. You should have seen my mail in 1988. People were not for Landry." (I didn't have to see the mail. I was hosting a nightly call-in radio show in 1988, and in December I got call after call, night after night, from fans insisting the game had passed Landry by and he should retire, after all. Somehow those people grew short memories when Jones removed Landry two months later, but I digress.)

"There were things Tom did I wasn't for" even in the glory days of the '70s, as Schramm recalled it. "But it was working. And even when it stopped working in the '80s, I just couldn't do it. We'd worked so long together and done so much together, I just could not bring myself to firing someone I'd been with [for] so much time, and we'd been so successful together."

The Cowboys' winning tradition may be Schramm's greatest legacy, but his greatest accomplishment may well have been figuring out a way to make a thirty-year partnership between himself, Landry, and Brandt successful. You've heard of the "Odd Couple"? You couldn't imagine an odder trio. None of the three had anything in common with the other two in terms of values or likes and dislikes except for one thing: the Cowboys.

How did Schramm make that work? By his own admission all three men were egotistical.

"It worked because we all stayed out of the other guy's business," Schramm said simply, as though any dolt should have figured it out. "I set down the rules in the beginning when we started the team. This was going to be Landry's area," gesturing to his right. "This was going to be Gil's area," with a wave to the left. And with a hearty laugh, "And all the rest was mine.

"Even when I disagreed with Landry, for instance, I could always understand his thinking. And we had a real strong chain of command with the Cowboys. And each of us respected the other's boundaries. That made it work. One of us wouldn't go into the other's area because we all understood no one would come into ours. I may have been the general manager, but I had no reason to bother Tom or Gil because they could deliver the goods. And they were loyal. We were all loyal to each other."

That loyalty made the organization work in a time when it was the right structure for success. And what success. All that winning, the championships, the highs so high and lows so low. What were Tex Schramm's favorite games, favorite seasons?

"I don't break 'em down to favorite games because you forget the games you won and you remember the games you lost," and with this, Schramm offered a glimpse into the competitive drive that kept him ahead of the pack for so many years. "The one thing I have always said when people have asked, 'What's the best thing that happened to you?' is being elected to the Hall of Fame. There just aren't very many people who can say that, and for me it's very, very important because it's the only thing I can point to after forty years in the league [he was with the Rams in Los Angeles in the 1950s] that other people recognize."

If you wanted to put words into his mouth, you could guess that Schramm's favorite game might have been the win over Miami in Super Bowl VI in New Orleans in January 1972. It was the team's first, and any Cowboys fan of long standing remembers the picture of a triumphant Schramm hoisting the Lombardi Trophy in one hand, absent only a caption, "I'm king of the world!" But if he remembered the losses, could he pick his least favorite of those?

That would probably be the 21–19 divisional playoff loss at home to the Rams in 1979. That loss kept the Cowboys from going to a third consecutive Super Bowl, and for Schramm it did even more. "We'd have been the team of that decade, and I knew that game meant we were giving that up," he recalled, and bitterness from it remained evident in him twenty-four years later. "That hurt like hell. And I wish we'd have won the damn Super Bowl the year before."

But the losses and the wins took second place in Tex Schramm's heart to the organization he helped build. "We had a lot of good people. Lots of them in the front office. Most of them a lot of people never heard of, but in those days everybody did everything, and some of them, like our ticket manager, Kay Lang . . . [were people] you couldn't replace very easily.

Tex Schramm hoists the Cowboys' first-ever Lombardi Trophy in January 1972.

"Virtually everybody in the organization had a drive to win, and they were loyal. We were in the entertainment business, and I enjoyed all of that. I enjoyed sharing credit in the success of some of the people who worked with us as announcers and writers. We all got along great, and we all felt like we were a part of something."

Schramm believed he'd have been successful in today's NFL, and he was probably right. For instance he's not cowed by the NFL's salary cap. He was a proponent of it years before it became part of the language, "because I knew we were in trouble. As long as I knew what the rules were, I felt like I could have played by them and won." Like Jerry Jones Schramm had no hesitation in testing the boundaries, one reason being that "if something was my idea, then I was on the line. I *had* to make it work."

Jerry Jones announced the induction of Tex Schramm (right) into the Ring of Honor at an April 2003 news conference at Texas Stadium.

But he was just as glad he came along when he did. "I'm so glad I was in the era I was in. I was in the end of the '40s, when football was a different thing. I was in the '50s when television was just starting to spread its roots and get going, and it was fun to be involved in that. With the Cowboys we brought computers into the game. We started the use of artificial turf in the NFL. A lot of things happened in that period."

The last big thrill in Tex Schramm's career came in March 2003 when Jerry Jones sent word to Schramm that the man who created the team's Ring of Honor would be inducted into it in the fall of 2003.

"It's the right thing to do," said Jones. "He's in the Hall of Fame, after all." When Schramm got the news on March 14, he was truly moved. "It's a tremendous honor," he admitted. "It's something that means a great deal to me." And on March 18, when Tex met with Jones at the team's Valley Ranch headquarters for lunch, it was his first return to the football compound he designed and created since his departure in 1989. Only a few people were present, and it was better that way. The old warhorse was home and clearly glad of it.

What fans couldn't see, but would have loved, came after lunch. Tex, who created the team's innovative television department to produce its own network of shows, met with the current crop of producers and editors. Realizing a golden chance, they peppered him with questions. Why did you do this, create that? He answered every question and would have stayed as long as they liked. It turned out to be Tex Schramm's last visit home.

The Zero Club

"I wouldn't want to belong to any club that would accept me as a member."

—Groucho Marx

The recorded history of professional football is enriched by the exploits of some of the great units the mention of whose very names evoke their legendary deeds: the Purple People Eaters, Fearsome Foursome, Steel Curtain, Doomsday Defense.

But recorded history is incomplete. It almost missed the Zero Club—which actually attests to the success of this hidden clan of crusty Dallas Cowboys. Being overlooked is what the Zero Club was all about.

Typical of everything it came to represent, the Zero Club existed before it was founded. When it was at its peak, it accomplished nothing, which was its aim. Today, it may or may not be alive and well. No one knows or much cares.

But perhaps only a franchise that produced the glamour of "America's Team" and five Super Bowl championships and that boasted the colorful characters the Cowboys did, especially in the '60s and '70s, could also have been home to such a stellar homage to the benefits of apathy.

To understand the Zero Club, which would greatly disappoint them all, one must first know its members. They weren't elected or appointed. They kind of just were.

What they also were, were three of the best, most intelligent, and most overlooked cogs in the Cowboys' earliest success.

The first of them was Blaine Nye, the spirit of the Zero Club. Nye was the Cowboys' fifth-round draft choice in 1968, an offensive guard from Stanford. He played with distinction for Dallas for nine seasons and was the only member of the group to be recognized as an all-star. Nye was named to the Pro Bowl in 1974 and in his final season, 1976. He was the anchor of three Super Bowl offensive lines.

There's no way to prove this, but I'll bet if you ran IQ tests on everyone who ever wore a Cowboys uniform, Blaine Nye would be among the top five. And his personality was the most volatile of the Zero Clubbers.

My earliest personal memory of Blaine was in his final season, which was my first as a Cowboys broadcaster, 1976. I joined the crew at midseason, and on road games I did color for play-by-play man Verne Lundquist. With five minutes to go in the game, I left the booth to go to the locker room, where I was to record four two-minute postgame interviews and send them back up the line to the booth. My second such outing, on November 21, came in an ugly 17–10 loss in the mud in Atlanta.

Win or lose, I had to get the interviews. None of the players yet knew me, nor I them. For some reason I had put Nye's name on the list that I gave public relations assistant Andy Anderson. When he approached Nye, I could hear from around the corner, "F___ them. They only want to talk to me after a game like that!? F___ KRLD!" I believe we substituted another player for Blaine that day.

Larry Cole was the Zero Clubber of the longest tenure with the Cowboys. He came along the same year as Nye, 1968, but as a sixteenth-round draft choice. Cole was, and is, a large lump of a man who never looked the part of an athlete. Big and pasty, he went from Granite Falls, Minnesota, to the Air Force Academy to the University of Hawaii. He and Nye met

It's Blaine Nye at the controls with Larry Cole along for the ride in a non–Zero Club moment in training camp.

at the Hula Bowl following their senior season, so they gravitated to one another when they found themselves in the same rookie class in Dallas in 1968. All Larry Cole did was forge a thirteen-year Cowboys career, during which he was overshadowed as a defensive lineman by not one, but two generations of all-stars: first Bob Lilly, Jethro Pugh and George Andrie; then Randy White, Harvey Martin, and Ed "Too Tall" Jones. But Cole made big play after big play. He returned three interceptions for touchdowns, tied for second in Dallas's career record book, and his tackle of Hall of Famer-to-be John Riggins set up one of the most dramatic wins in Cowboys history, over Washington in December 1979. The fact that Larry Cole could have such a distinguished career and escape the notice of so many is the very essence of the Zero Club.

In point of fact, whenever Nye and Cole got together, the Zero Club was in session. But it never took any formal shape until it added its third and final member, Pat Toomay, a brainy defensive end drafted in the sixth round from Vanderbilt in 1970. Toomay played in Dallas through 1974 before moving on to Buffalo, Tampa Bay, and Oakland. In true Zero Club fashion, he found himself a member of the Bucs' record-setting 0–14 expansion team in 1976.

Pat Toomay was an uncommon intellectual in a game not often noted for deep thinking. (My first encounter with Pat came after a game at Texas Stadium in 1971, the year the Zero Club was born. I was just another young, naive reporter in a postgame locker room crowd, and I approached him for a comment on how the evening had gone. "Well," I remember Toomay musing thoughtfully, "as Nietzsche said. . . . " And being just a year out of school myself and not being accustomed to having football players quote nineteenth-century German philosophers, I remember thinking, "This dummy

Aloha

Larry Cole is one of just five players from Hawaii to play for the Cowboys. The others: receiver Golden Richards (1973-78), running back Gary Allen (1983-84), kicker Kerry Brady (1987), and tackle Mark Tuinei (1983-97).

doesn't even know how to pronounce Ray Nitschke's name." That intellect accounts for his success as a writer, at which he makes his living today in upstate New York. For many, the first public recounting of the Zero Club came in Toomay's classic football memoir, *The Crunch*, published in 1975.

But Toomay today recalls the beginnings of the Zero Club as though it were just yesterday. "The Zero Club," he says, "existed in a kind of quasistate, a nameless state. My second year [1971], we had the first Saturday night of training camp [in Thousand Oaks, California] off. Cliff Harris and Charlie Waters got all dressed up and went out. Lee Roy [Jordan] and Walt Garrison had taken them under their wing.

"So there it is, Saturday night, and I'm sitting in my dorm room at Cal Lutheran College with nothing to do. I started wandering down the hall, and from somewhere down the hallway I could hear the muted sound of a TV set. I walked toward it. When I got to the room, I propped open the door. On the far wall was a long window that had been taped up with a tinfoil covering in order to eliminate any life-giving sunlight that might seep in.

"On the far bed lay Larry Cole, large and pasty white like a corpse. Except that he was snoring and blind to the world. On the near bed was Blaine, all blue and lifeless and apparently asleep. The TV wasn't tuned to a channel. It was just snow, and the horizontal hold didn't work, so it was all just gray and rolling. Blaine opened one eye, looked at me, and said, 'Welcome to the Zero Club.' There was an air of languor that existed as a permanent state in their room."

It wasn't that the Zero Club never wanted to go anywhere, Toomay said. "It's just that no one ever invited us." And on the rare occasions when the Zero Clubbers tried to emerge from their shells, the results were predictable. All three remember the story that Toomay tells best: "One time we decided to go to a movie, but we had no car. We had to bum a ride into town from some rookie who was taking his girlfriend out. Imagine how humiliating that was, us being cool guys that he looked up to. So we get a ride to the movie, but we never bothered to check on what the movie was. We wound up seeing *How to Frame a Figg* with Don Knotts. There was no one else there. Literally, we were the only ones. Cole farted during the movie and we walked back to camp."

Nye, who today runs the Stanford Consulting Group in the San Francisco Bay area, sums it up this way: "Some people are famous and some are infamous. We were un-famous."

Or at least they might have been until Frank Luksa came along.

Luksa today lolls in semiretirement as a sports columnist for the *Dallas Morning News*. In the 1970s he covered the Cowboys for the now-defunct *Dallas Times-Herald*, and it was in that capacity that he fell upon the Zero Club.

"I stumbled on the Zero Club by accident," he remembers, and truly, only by accident could the Zero Club have possibly been discovered. "I was wandering around the dormitory in Thousand Oaks. Maybe I had an interview with Toomay or Nye or Cole, I don't know. But I came upon the room where the three of them were congregated, and a meeting was in progress. Of course nothing was happening,

Pat Toomay contemplates another tough day at the office.

and they explained to me that nothing ever did happen. That was the beauty of the thing.

"One of them said, 'Welcome to the Zero Club,' and I said, 'What's that?' So they had to explain. Blaine Nye was the president, Pat Toomay was the vice president, and Cole was the dynamic social chairman. None of those offices had any function, of course. It was all a put-on about their anonymity, and they carried it off with great cheer, especially after they started getting some publicity. I used to do an annual column, usually my last one from training camp, about what the Zero Club did this year. Which was always nothing, or as little as possible."

As Toomay outlined in *The Crunch* and recalls again now, "We just tried to make a virtue of our liability. We figured out it was like Joseph Heller wrote in *Catch-22*: There was a useful purpose in cultivating boredom. It can extend your career, because the more bored you are, the more time slows down, and the longer you can last."

Sometimes the Zero Club made grand plans, which of course it never carried out. "Once," Luksa remembers, "they made plans to all get up and perform a task. The task was to take Cole down to a tattoo parlor and have a tattoo put on him that was going to say, 'Born to Raise Wheat.' Of course they never got around to it. They were hilarious to be around, listening to them talk about all the things they didn't do."

And when they did do things, they tried to lower themselves to the occasion. All remembered the time the Cowboys were about to play the vaunted Steelers, and Nye would be facing a head-to-head matchup with the great Pittsburgh tackle, Mean Joe Greene. In a pregame interview KRLD's Frank Glieber asked Nye, "Blaine, what will it be like to go up against the quickest, biggest, toughest guy in the league? How do you plan on handling him? Isn't this what pro football is all about, getting to prove yourself against the greatest of the great?"

"Personally," Nye answered, "I'd rather play a dog any day."

"Don't the two of you match up well?" Glieber tried again.

"Yeah," said Blaine. "His strengths match up perfectly against my weaknesses."

Cole, who has become one of the Dallas–Fort Worth area's most successful home builders, once ran for the city council in the suburb of Bedford. That very act seemed to be at odds with the purpose of the Zero Club, but as Cole later explained to Toomay, "I got just what I wanted: defeat."

The very notion that Luksa would publicize the Zero Club in print seems to contradict its existence, yet had he not done so, hardly anyone would have noticed. Toomay recalls, "Frank did subvert the purpose of the Zero Club by writing about it, so he became the official scribe. I don't remember how he justified writing about it. He had some clever rationale. I think we justified it by thinking that if he wanted to risk his career by associating with us, that kind of stayed in the spirit of the thing.

"When Frank wrote about us, nobody noticed and nobody cared. Well, actually, that's not true. Through the years I've heard from people who said they really enjoyed the stories. I

Author, Author

Pat Toomay is not the only former Cowboy to be published. Receiver Pete Gent (1964-68) wrote the novel *North Dallas Forty* which later became a movie, starring Mac Davis and Kris Kristofferson.

hear from servicemen who come across them on the Internet. Just got an e-mail from Italy. People who say their spirits were lifted by those columns."

Nye remembers that "after Frank wrote one of his stories about it, people noticed. Even Coach [Tom] Landry came by one day during practice and said, 'How's the club?' Even Tom thought it was funny. But we didn't mind Frank writing about it. We took all the publicity we could get. We had fun with it."

All the publicity they could get still wasn't much. When the Cowboys went to their second consecutive Super Bowl after the 1971 season, the three sat together, of course, on Media Day. As Cole recalls, "All the press were gathered around the big stars, Lilly and Staubach and so forth. No one interviewed us. It wasn't that we refused to talk. No one wanted to talk to us. After a while I looked at the other two guys and said, 'Why are we here?' But we had to stay."

As you might expect, as soon as a group as undistinguished as the Zero Club got a little notoriety, it found itself with the one thing it could not abide: people who wanted to join.

"They did seem to embrace the attention, but only if it was directed at them," Luksa says. "If someone else made inquiries, they were automatically disqualified."

"As time went on," Toomay agrees, "people exhibited some interest in joining the Zero Club, which kind of put them out of the running automatically. Jim Arneson [a guard drafted in the twelfth round from Arizona in 1973] was so desperate to be in the Zero Club he couldn't stand it."

Nye remembers the nascent membership of center John Fitzgerald, an outstanding Cowboy from 1971 to 1980. "Fitz wanted to be in, but he couldn't stand the pace." Luksa recalls receiver Ron Sellers, who was "too active or too energetic. Anyone like that was out."

Cole had the best nominee who truly could have been a Zero Clubber had he come around a little earlier: tackle Andy Frederick, a fifth-round pick in 1977. "Andy's more Zero Club than I am." Frederick lasted until 1981, possibly because no one ever knew he was there. But by that time Nye and Toomay were gone, and Cole wasn't the type to carry on by himself.

"We were all pretty self-effacing guys," Cole says now. "I never did the talking. Blaine always had the quick one-liners, and Pat's a writer. But I seemed to be the symbol of the thing.

I always aspired to be a crusty old fart, and I think I've done a pretty good job of that."

Nor, by the way, could anyone else have become the official chronicler of the Zero Club besides Luksa. "Others tried to write about them," he says with some small pride (but not too much), "but they could never capture the essence. There were plenty of times I fit right in with their lifestyle, their pace."

Would the Zero Club have been so interesting (no offense intended, fellas) had the players involved not been so productive? Who knows? But the fact is, far from being zeroes, Nye, Cole, and Toomay were three of the most intelligent and interesting people who ever played in Dallas. They were also all three excellent players. In the *Cowboys Official Weekly* in 1999, publisher Russ Russell reported in a feature on the Zero Club that former Landry assistant Ermal Allen had once said Cole regularly graded out higher than any other player on defense.

As for intelligence Cole has proven his business acumen, Nye holds multiple degrees from Stanford, and Toomay is a graduate of Vanderbilt and was a published author even during his playing days.

Zero Clubbers Pat Toomay (67) and Larry Cole (63) look to the offense for help.

All were iconoclasts. Cole recalls, "We spent our time, especially at training camp, reading and doing things that typical football players might not do. We loved to argue. I would always take the business position, and Blaine would always take the labor position, and Toomay would take the liberal college professor argument. In fact, back then, none of us had agents. Blaine loved to get into all the facets of contract negotiations, and I hated the process. I always waited until he went in and did his deal, and then I went in and said, 'Give me whatever you're giving him.' Although as he got older and got a lot of money, Nye became a heck of a Republican."

To the observation that none of the Zeros was a zero, Nye dryly notes, "Well, the jury's still out on that. It was pretty apparent that being smart and cool were not related."

So what of the Zero Club now? They still stay in touch. Cole continues to build homes and has been traveling to auto-graph shows with Bob Lilly. Nye consults in northern California and dotes on his family. (A son, Matt, has graduated from the Naval Academy, where he played football in Dad's tradition. And in some strange Zero Clublike metaphysical "six degrees of separation," Nye's daughter Missy is married to Tom Whitenight, a college teammate of former Cowboys quarterback Troy Aikman.) Toomay has written two books and contributes columns to ESPN.com.

Luksa has beaten them down the road to doing nothing, but even he writes a column a week. Not in many years, though, about the Zero Club. Not since December 1985. The previous year, on the occasion of the Cowboys' Twenty-Fifth Anniversary Silver Soiree, Luksa wrote that none of the three had been included on the Cowboys all-time team: "Thus, the goal toward which the Zero Club struggled all these years has been reached. Each and every one is finally and completely, totally obscure."

Captains America

Every family has some dysfunction, whether it's yours or the folks next door. And in every Partridge Family, there's likely a Jack Osbourne hiding somewhere.

Because of the sheer strength of Coach Tom Landry's personality, the early Dallas Cowboys were assigned his straight-arrow mantle. That's why Pete Gent's book, and the movie made from it, *North Dallas Forty*, were received with such interest. That's why Cowboys players' human foibles were greeted with such headline-grabbing alarm.

Beginning in 1978, when NFL Films labeled the Super Bowl champions "America's Team," Cowboy haters everywhere were quick with an "Aha!" whenever a player ran into trouble. And goodness knows, through the years there have been times when it seemed like trouble was all dressed up and out looking for a Dallas Cowboy. Even a former Cowboy would do. No one, no team could be that good on and off the field.

Never mind the fact that trouble has just as frequently found a Bengal or a Packer or a Redskin or a Panther. For better or worse, since the mid-1960s, the Dallas Cowboys have had an image, and there is always someone ready to volunteer to prove that image false.

That's why it's so hard for all those people to swallow the fact that two of Dallas's most shining lights have been Real Heroes. Not just football stars put on a pedestal by adoring fans, but real American military heroes. Of the dozens of products of America's service academies, Army, Navy, and Air

Force, to reach the NFL, the Dallas Cowboys have had the two who made the biggest contributions to their football teams. Call them Captain(s) America: Roger Staubach and Chad Hennings.

This is not to say that Staubach and Hennings were better soldiers or better Americans than anyone else, certainly not better than the other military men who have come before and after them in the NFL. It is to say that maybe it's just a coincidence, but the two most dramatic contributors to professional football from America's military played their entire careers for Dallas.

First, a little perspective. Hennings played for the Cowboys from 1992 through 2000, after winning the Outland Trophy as college football's top interior lineman at Air Force. He was a key component in the defensive line for three Super Bowl champions and a full-time starter for five years and part of a sixth. Staubach was a Cowboy from 1969 to 1979, after winning the Heisman and Maxwell Trophies at Navy. He led Dallas to four Super Bowls (winning two), was inducted into the team's exclusive Ring of Honor in 1983, and was elected to the Pro Football Hall of Fame in 1985.

Hennings is one of just four Air Force Academy grads to appear in a regular-season NFL game. Steve Russ was briefly a linebacker in Denver, Bryce Fisher has been a defensive lineman for Buffalo and St. Louis, and linebacker Chris Gizzi has played for Green Bay.

Through the 2002 season eighteen men had played football at the Naval Academy (some did not graduate) and matriculated to the NFL. Other than Staubach, the best pros were probably receiver Phil McConkey, who had some sparkling moments for the Giants in the 1980s, and running back Napoleon McCallum, a Raider in 1986 and from 1990

Former Navy star Roger Staubach (left) with rookie Chad Hennings (95) from Air Force during Hennings' rookie training camp in 1992.

through 1994. Defensive tackle Bob Kuberski was a Packer from 1995 to 1998; offensive lineman Mike Wahle has been a Packer since 1998. Heisman Trophy winner Joe Bellino carried the ball for the Patriots from 1965 through 1967. Most of the other Midshipmen played in the league for no more than a couple of years between 1925 and 1960.

In its 2002 Season Kickoff press release, the NFL listed twenty-three Army Cadets who appeared in the pros. Heisman Trophy winner Glenn Davis is the most notable. He was a

Ram in 1950 and 1951. The longest tenured was lineman Bob Mischak, who appeared for the Giants, New York Titans, and Raiders from 1958 to 1965.

Those are the facts, ma'am, and just the facts. And so is this: No service academy product had an NFL career remotely approaching what Captains America did for America's Team, neither as well nor as long.

Staubach, of course, came first. Current Cowboys fans may not know how close he was to having been a Kansas City Chief instead.

NFL draft rules were different in the 1960s. You could select a player as a "future," which Dallas did with Roger in 1964. He had won the Heisman as a junior in 1963. The AFL Chiefs, owned by Dallasite Lamar Hunt, also spent a future pick on Staubach in 1964.

The pride that has propelled his entire life wells up even now when Staubach, sitting in a conference room of The Staubach Company, a real-estate services outfit, recalls that Dallas picked him in the tenth round, "and there were something like seventeen rounds [actually twenty], so it wasn't a throwaway deal. Kansas City picked me as a future later on. When I was a junior at the Naval Academy, I felt I could play quarterback in the National Football League. I hadn't been doing it that long. I didn't play quarterback until my senior year in high school actually. Rick Forzano tried to get me to play safety at Navy, but I had dislocated my left shoulder playing baseball. My sophomore year is when I started developing into a pretty good throwing quarterback.

"But I wasn't yet thinking of the NFL. I knew I had a commitment for four years, and I still had my senior year to go, so everyone was thinking, 'Well, he's got five years to go.' But right after I graduated, when I was an ensign, I played in the

College All-Star Game. I had three weeks in that camp, and that's when pro scouts really knew that I could throw. We had some great players on that team. I was there with [Craig] Morton, Bob Timberlake, and John Huarte. We had Bob Hayes, [Gale] Sayers, [Dick] Butkus, and there were scouts there every day watching the guys they'd drafted. It was almost like going to a combine today.

Academy Awards

Roger Staubach is one of five service academy winners of college football's Heisman Trophy. The others: Felix "Doc" Blanchard, Army, 1945; Glenn Davis, Army, 1946; Pete Dawkins, Army, 1958; and Joe Bellino, Navy, 1960. Chad Hennings is one of only two academy winners of the Outland Trophy. The other: Army's Joe Steffy in 1947.

"After that, Lamar Hunt came to see me. He wanted to sign me to a contract saying that if I ever left the service, I'd play for the Chiefs. Lenny Dawson was their quarterback at the time. Hunt came to our house in Annapolis. I was stationed at the academy for six months. Marianne and I had just gotten married, and I'm thinking, 'Gee, Lamar Hunt, the owner of the Kansas City Chiefs, and he wants to come see me!' He had dinner at our house. He said, 'I want to draw up a contract, if you'd be interested.' And I said, 'Jeez, yeah, it sounds great to me.' I talked to Captain Paul Borden, a Navy legal officer, and he said there didn't sound like there was anything wrong with it. So [Hunt] came by a second time with the outline of a contract. It was basically to pay me ten thousand bucks, $500 a month while I was in the service, and then $50,000 if I left the service. It was really $100,000, but it was deferred, so it was present-value $50,000. Here I am an ensign making $250 a month.

"Captain Borden said it sounded fine. He said, 'Legally, you can do this.' But he said, 'Dallas also drafted you,' and I said, 'Well, they haven't talked to me.' So he called Dallas. There was a track coach at the academy who knew Gil Brandt [Cowboys personnel director], so maybe he said to Captain Borden something like, 'Hey, you ought to call Dallas.' Which he did. This was a weekend where the Cowboys happened to be playing the Eagles, so [Captain Borden] went to the Eagles–Dallas game and actually met Tex [Schramm], Clint [Murchison, the club's owner], and Gil.

"He sat down with Tex and Gil and gave them the same deal, and they said, 'We'll match that in a second.' So he called me and I said, 'Hey, that's great.' I called Lamar Hunt and told him personally, and he was really disappointed. He said he'd negotiate a better deal, but I didn't want to get into that. Dallas was in the NFL, and I didn't want to get into a bidding contest."

In 1965 the AFL had signed Joe Namath, and they were, as Staubach says, "making traction." But Roger had grown up in Cincinnati, following the Cleveland Browns and the NFL, and he went with the more established league. What Cowboys fan knew the team owed its first great era to the intervention of the late Captain Paul Borden?

With Chad Hennings it was a little different. In many ways Hennings was Schramm and Brandt's parting gift to the Cowboys, although they didn't know that when they selected him in the eleventh round in 1988. By then there was no such thing as a future pick. Chad had been an all-American and the winner of the Outland Trophy as a senior in 1987, and many scouts felt he would have gone high in the first round but for his service commitment. Instead of twenty rounds, as when Staubach was chosen, the draft had been pared to twelve rounds. In Staubach's era future picks were common. By 1988 there was much more pressure for draft choices to make quick contributions. There was also no college all-star game any more. So, although Staubach had a chance to prove he could compete with the best pro prospects, Hennings was taken more on faith. What was the cost if an eleventh-round pick didn't make it, after all? And because of the success they had with Staubach, Schramm and Brandt had a better sense of the upside than most.

While he was putting together his eye-popping senior season at Air Force, did Hennings have doubts about getting a chance to play in the NFL? "A simple answer? Yes and no," Hennings says, flashing that Iowa farm boy smile that made him so appealing to fans. "I always knew in the back of my mind that I was going to have an opportunity to play. That's why [while on active duty] I continued to lift weights and continued to stay in shape and gain weight and gain strength and whatnot. But by the same token, I was flying jets. I was flying jets in the active-duty air force, flying in the Gulf War, and flying in Operation Provide Comfort. Doing that, I didn't really know if I'd have the chance, because I was looking at an eight-year military commitment and being thirty-two years old before I even had the chance to get out and play. You don't see many thirty-two-year-old rookies in the NFL. But for me it was just a patience and a faith thing, and I'd let God work it out."

Although Staubach had almost fallen into the Cowboys' laps because of the intervention of a third party, it was the team that reached out to Hennings. In 1989, just after buying the team that February, owner–general manager Jerry Jones called Hennings at Sheppard Air Force Base in Wichita Falls, Texas,

Chad Hennings (95) made an impact when he left the air force for the Cowboys.

a two-hour drive from Dallas. Hennings was in pilot training there, and Jones helped make it possible for Hennings to come to Texas Stadium to watch the team play in a couple of games. Although Hennings told Jones he had made a commitment to flying, Jones wanted to make sure of the options that were available. He contacted Dallasite Bob Strauss, a political insider of long standing in Washington, D.C., and later U.S. ambassador to Russia, and had Strauss check with contacts in the Department of Defense about the possibility of an early release. Strauss learned that there was virtually none. Jones told Jill Lieber of *Sports Illustrated* magazine in July 1992, "I

felt that Chad's visibility with the Cowboys would be a great trade-off with the air force to forgo his commitment. But Chad always had mixed emotions, and I sensed that he wasn't pining away for the Cowboys."

Nor had Staubach. Both men were driven to succeed at whatever they did. Both were, and are, patriots before they were football players. And both felt honored to serve their country in time of great peril.

For Staubach that time was during the war in Vietnam. After six months at the Naval Academy and six months in supply school, Staubach was sent to Vietnam for a year in the early fall of 1966. He was a naval support officer in Da Nang and Chu Lai, not, as he puts it, "out getting shot at. I was on shore duty supporting the Marines, actually."

In fact Staubach might have been a Marine. "I was partially color blind. That's how I ended up in the supply corps," he recalls. "I didn't have the passion to fly. I didn't know exactly what I wanted to do. But the Marines were recruiting me hard. I had a very important job in Vietnam. In effect I was running a business. I had 120 people working for me, off-loading ships. But I told a reporter for *Stars and Stripes* one time that I didn't feel like I was doing enough, that I was sitting on the sidelines. That really ticked off one admiral, who told me, 'Now you're affecting all those people who are in a support role.' And it was wrong of me to do that."

But if Staubach didn't have what he calls "the rush of combat, of being out there and being shot at," Hennings certainly did in the Gulf War. In fact, in terms of what many little boys dream about, Chad Hennings hit the jackpot: "I got to fly jets and play in the NFL."

Which dream did Hennings enjoy most? Flying combat missions in a war or playing in the Super Bowl?

"All the extraneous stuff aside, flying jets," he says with little hesitation, and a questioner must marvel at the very choice the big man never had to make. "It's not even close. It's like going to a Super Bowl every day. Every mission that you step out, you're flying in a high-performance aircraft, shooting a 30-millimeter Gatling gun that shoots 4,000 rounds a minute, often at static tanks from more than 15,000 feet out. The true sense of a man, the hunter-gatherer, that defines it. Whereas football is a gladiator, it's very demanding physically—and flying is, too—but you can fly a heck of a lot longer than you can play in the NFL. They [the Super Bowls] were fun, but all in all, flying. I believe that's the first time I've ever said that to anybody."

That being the case, where might Chad Hennings be today had it not been for football? "I'd probably be a lieutenant colonel someplace as an operations officer in some squadron, grooming myself to be the next chief of staff of the air force." Modesty forces Hennings to chuckle, but only a little.

So any regrets that he gave that all up for the NFL? "No, no regrets," he says quickly. "Looking back on it, the whole experience I had is like a fairy tale. Every kid wants to have the opportunity to fly airplanes or to play a professional sport. If I could do it all over again, I'd do it the same way."

With both men the Cowboys were smart enough to see what they had even before they had it. In Staubach's case he knew he had a four-year hitch to serve. But at the time the Cowboys had Don Meredith (a man for whom Staubach maintains immense respect and affection) at quarterback, and

After his Navy and Cowboys days, Roger Staubach (left) still had connections. Here, at a Cowboys function with former teammate Cliff Harris and a young Texas businessman, George W. Bush. Whatever became of him?

Landry believed young quarterbacks should serve at least a four-year apprenticeship anyway. So Brandt started sending Staubach film to study, and in his third year in the service, he took a two-week leave from the Navy to attend training camp in Thousand Oaks, California. That was in 1968, and Staubach remembers, "I had a really good camp. That's when I knew I was going to play professional football. That's the moment I knew, when I left that camp. I ran well, threw well, and they knew that I could be an NFL quarterback. Actually,

Coach Landry let me take the playbook back to Pensacola with me. When I left, people told me there's no way he would have given me that playbook if he didn't think I could play football."

In the spring of 1969, Staubach took another two-week leave and attended a quarterback school in Dallas. "I was in quarterback school with Morton and Meredith and myself. Jerry Rhome had just been traded to Cleveland. Meredith was great. He was as nice as he could be to me."

A few weeks later, done with his active duty commitment, Staubach packed up the family dog to drive home to Cincinnati, where his wife and three daughters had gone. Before he left, "I got a call from Curt Moser [then-Cowboys public relations director], who said, 'I just wanted you to know, Don Meredith announced his retirement today. You're our backup quarterback.' " Staubach remembers getting beaten to a pulp in a rookie scrimmage against the Oakland Raiders. "They took me to the doctor and found out I had blood in my urine and two broken transverse processes in my back. So our veterans come in, and I'm in shorts and I can hardly walk. But Landry didn't trade for anybody. He kept me as the backup quarterback. That's how important those two weeks in camp were the year before."

In Hennings's case, although there had been no evidence of an early out from the air force in 1989, things changed after the Gulf War. "After the war, at the end of '91, beginning of '92, our military underwent an across-the-board reduction in force, a RIF," he says. "I was now able to have not only a year of my pilot training commitment waived, but also twenty-four months off the service academy commitment, something they had never done before. That's what started the ball rolling. I contacted my agent [Jack Mills] who had talked to Tex Schramm and Gil Brandt back in '88. He asked if the Cowboys were still interested in me. That's when I flew back from England (where Hennings was stationed at an RAF base in Bentwaters) to Dallas for a workout. Flew back on a Friday evening, worked out Saturday morning. 'Yes, we want you. How soon can you get out?' Flew back to London, put my papers in, and within three weeks I was in Dallas. I got here on Memorial Day of '92."

Sounds like that quick overnight transatlantic workout went pretty well, huh? "It's a pretty funny story. We met at a hotel with Bob Ackles, the personnel director, Jerry, Stephen Jones [the Cowboys vice-president]. We sat around and talked about my war experiences that night, and then I had to get up in the morning and do a workout. I was expecting to work out just for Mike Woicik [the strength coach at the time] and Butch [Davis, then the Cowboys defensive coordinator and now head coach of the Cleveland Browns]. But they had the whole coaching staff there, a couple of reporters. I'm thinking, 'Holy cow, what the heck is this? I haven't run a 40 in five years.' I ran a 40-yard dash, did some pass-rushing drills and some other drills, and a bench press. I was still on England time, a differential of about seven hours. I was running on adrenaline. I hadn't slept in twenty-four hours, and I'm going through this workout. It was interesting. I ended up having some pretty decent times." Apparently. In that 1992 *Sports Illustrated* article, Jill Lieber wrote that Mills had also contacted the Denver Broncos, who were interested in a trade for Hennings had the Cowboys not liked what they saw, but that once Coach Jimmy Johnson got a look at Hennings, he told Jones, "Forget about trading this guy."

Although their situations were far from analogous, there is little doubt in Hennings' mind that Roger Staubach helped pave the way for him. "There were different branches of service, different sides of the ball, different positions, that whole thing," Hennings agrees. "But the thing I had in my favor was that there was precedent set with Roger for having done it and having had success. There might have been a little more pressure on me because of that. I mean, he was a Hall of Fame quarterback. He was Captain Comeback. He was The Man."

For his part Staubach wishes he could have done more with and for Hennings. "He's a great guy. I tried to tell him a few things he might expect, but he was ready for it. You could tell it right away."

And not surprisingly, Staubach also feels both of them were ready to be Captains America because of their military training. "A lot of the responsibilities you have as a leader in the military are like the responsibilities when you have a bunch of guys in the huddle. At the end of the day, people are looking for someone to make decisions or to believe in. The military teaches you that. You have to make decisions, and there are people depending on the decisions you make."

It's pretty obvious two generations of Cowboys leadership made good decisions on Roger Staubach and Chad Hennings.

Regular Greatness

The best questions are the ones that have no right answers.

I've been broadcasting Dallas Cowboys games for some twenty-five years, and I'm frequently asked to name my favorite game. It's impossible to say. I've broadcast four Super Bowls. Some of them weren't as good as some regular-season games, although in the grand scheme of things they may have meant more. And how do you single out one regular-season game as the best the Cowboys have ever played? For crying out loud, they've played 650 of them, and I didn't see all of those, although at 364 and counting, I'm in on more than 50 percent. That may not qualify me as an expert, but it does give me room for an opinion.

After 364 regular-season games, they start to run together. But a few do stand out. The season opener in 1999 was a thriller: in Washington, a back-and-forth game against the Cowboys' most bitter rival, won 41–35 in overtime on a long pass from Troy Aikman to Rocket Ismail. Head coach and offensive coordinator Chan Gailey had been working on that play all summer.

The Cowboys have played some wonderfully entertaining Thanksgiving Day games. One of the best was the 1994 comeback win over Green Bay, 42–31, because it was highlighted by the ultimate day in the sun of one of my favorites, quarterback Jason Garrett. Garrett was third team behind Aikman and Rodney Peete in 1994, but they were both injured that day, and Jason celebrated the holiday by drilling the Packers for 311 yards, most of them in the second half, and two touchdowns.

And for drama and excitement, it doesn't get much better than the season finale against the Giants in 1993. With playoff home-field advantage and a desperately needed first-round bye at stake, the Cowboys got a performance for the ages from Emmitt Smith, playing much of the day with a separated shoulder, and an overtime field goal from Eddie Murray to win 16–13. Thanks largely to that win, twenty-eight days later the Cowboys won their second consecutive Super Bowl.

But as great as those games were, they are runners-up on my list. If I had one game to watch again, it would be the December 16, 1979, game against the Washington Redskins at Texas Stadium. You've probably seen the NFL Films highlights. Dallas beat Washington 35–34. That game was Regular Greatness.

Imagine the scene: It's cold, around thirty-five degrees, and a little windy. Kickoff was at 3:00 P.M., so the game was finished in chill darkness. The Cowboys had been to two straight Super Bowls, but a bizarre combination of injuries and defections had made them a different team. Still, they entered the final weekend of the season 10–5, tied for first with the hated Washingtons. The Redskins had won the first meeting just four weeks earlier, 34–20, at RFK Stadium. In their second year under Coach Jack Pardee, they came to Texas looking for a knockout punch. Everything was at stake. The winner claimed the NFC East Division title and potentially a bye in the wild-card round of the playoffs the next week. And for Washington the stakes were greater. If they lost, a combination of tiebreakers would probably mean they would miss the playoffs altogether.

Acrimonious words flowed back and forth during the week leading up to the game, culminating in a funeral wreath being delivered to Cowboys defensive end Harvey Martin's locker before the game. It was unsigned, but Harvey had no question who had sent it. (Its emanation from Washington was never proved, and there has been plenty of speculation that it was an inside job, sent by someone in the Dallas camp to fire up the emotional Martin. If so, it worked.)

The combination of those factors alone, against the backdrop of the Cowboys–Redskins rivalry, set the stage for a memorable football game. But no one could have predicted the tension, the emotional roller coaster that would ensue.

To illustrate the hill the Cowboys climbed that day, we must first examine what they didn't have. They began the year with a key component from their back-to-back Super Bowl teams missing: Defensive end Ed Jones stunned the club after the 1978 season when he announced what turned out to be a one-year retirement to pursue a career as a boxer. John Dutton, who had been a Pro Bowl end with the Baltimore Colts, was obtained in a midseason trade only because he wasn't playing for Baltimore; he'd been a holdout and was sitting at home in Nebraska. It took Dutton awhile to grasp the defense, to say nothing of getting in football shape.

Thomas Henderson, the mercurial linebacker who had been a key part of three Super Bowl teams, got himself fired by Coach Tom Landry ten games into the season. And the Cowboys played the whole year without Pro Bowl safety Charlie Waters, who had torn up his knee in a preseason game in Seattle. In fact Waters spent the game with me in the radio booth as a color analyst/cheerleader.

To make matters worse Waters' replacement, Randy Hughes, missed the game with a bad shoulder, and star running back Tony Dorsett was unavailable because of a shoulder injury suffered the week before in Philadelphia. And in a development that is pretty funny in retrospect but wasn't a bit amusing at the time, the club's (then) career receiving leader, Drew Pearson, was also limited with a self-inflicted injury suffered two weeks before: Pearson had hurt his knee spiking the ball after a touchdown against the Giants.

There has been no more competitive Cowboy than quarterback Roger Staubach, and having such a silly injury deny him his best receiver in the biggest game of the year didn't sit well with number 12. But he had to adjust. The Cowboys, it seemed, had been adjusting all year.

And they had to start adjusting in this game right from the get-go. Running back Ron Springs fumbled but recovered the opening kickoff. Starting for Dorsett, he fumbled again on the second play of the game, but this one was recovered by Washington's Brad Dusek at the Dallas 34. On a play that would prove prophetic, defensive tackle Larry Cole sacked Redskins quarterback Joe Theismann on third and goal from the 3, and Mark Moseley kicked a field goal.

On the next possession, after the Cowboys made two first downs, sure-handed fullback Robert Newhouse lost another fumble, and Dusek recovered again, at the Redskins' 48. Three plays and a Dallas personal foul later, Theismann scooted around right end for a touchdown. The first quarter was half gone and the Redskins led 10–0.

And that was the good news.

After an exchange of punts, the Cowboys had to kick a second time. Washington ended the first quarter with the ball at its 20, overcame a second and 21 after a sack by Dutton, and got running back Benny Malone loose for a 45-yard scoring catch from Theismann a minute and a half into the second period. It was 17–0 Washington, and Dallas was staggered.

And listening to Staubach all these years later, you can tell this was not the right game for all these mistakes. "It was a bitter rivalry," he recalls, and even now his eyes narrow and his shoulders square a little at the thought. "They didn't like us and we didn't like them. And Jack Pardee had taken over from [former coach George] Allen, and Pardee was a former player there who hated the Cowboys."

But as the day would prove, there was no quit in this battered Dallas team. In fact this game and the winning of it are more remarkable in review when you also recall the ones who played hurt. In addition to

Hail to the Chief

Cowboys head coaches' records versus Washington: Tom Landry, 32–24–2 (including 0–2 in playoffs); Jimmy Johnson, 5–5; Barry Switzer, 4–4; Chan Gailey, 4–0; Dave Campo, 5–1.

the litany of key performers who missed the game, Randy White, the All-Pro defensive tackle, was limping around with two bad insteps. All-Pro safety Cliff Harris does not look back on the game fondly because he played it with a torn plantar fascia, a debilitating foot injury that he calls "the most painful injury I had in my career."

Still, Waters, ever the optimist, chirped his faith from the radio booth all day. "I really believed the Cowboys still had a chance the whole time," he says, which is why he spent the fourth quarter yelling at me, "You gotta believe, Brad!" "I think all of us as players always had that. I never questioned that somehow, something was going to happen that would give us a chance. Roger did that for us an awful lot, and our defensive team seemed to always be getting the ball back."

But at 17–0 a minute and a half into the second quarter,

they weren't exactly brimming with confidence down on the field. Running back Preston Pearson, as great a third-down receiving specialist as the franchise ever had, wound up enjoying a typical (for him) day of making big, clutch plays. But at this point, no Cowboy was doing anything.

"We were getting the crap kicked out of us," Pearson, still lean and lanky as in his playing days, recalls. "Physically, mentally, coaching, and they were over there enjoying the hell out of it."

Perhaps the Cowboys' saving grace was that they got behind early, because they had plenty of time to catch up; there was no need yet to deviate from the game plan. Staubach led a 70-yard, thirteen-play drive that used up more than eight minutes. Runs, short passes to the backs, no play longer than 10 yards, and the Cowboys made four first downs along the way. Springs plunged in from a yard out to make it 17–7 with slightly more than four and a half minutes left in the half. The defense forced a punt, and Dallas took over at its 15 with 1:48 before intermission. And then, here came Staubach.

Twenty-one yards to Tony Hill, 9 to Springs, 12 and 13 to Hill, 20 to Drew Pearson on his gimpy knee for his only catch of the day. Then three incompletions sandwiched around a holding penalty. Third and 20 at the Washington 26 with fifteen seconds left in the half.

Let's let Preston Pearson tell it.

"Obviously, we needed to have something there to shut down the Washington Redskins' thought processes, because we could hear. Guys were talking trash on the field, and it was boiling.

"That particular play, we really didn't have too many options. Drew was hurt, and when I would come in on third down situations, they were doubling and tripling me, *except* when we got into that situation there, [then] they would go into man coverage with Mark Murphy, a safety. We knew if I moved out of the backfield up to the line, he would be covering me. I would be in the slot.

"Now, Tom [Landry] was good at helping me set up moves. Tom's brain was always being prepared, studying film. And he told me this guy would bite on an inside move, especially if he was lined up to my inside, which he was. So we knew we had the situation. After that it was just a matter of executing what we had practiced that week. I just had to go at least 10 yards to sell it. My thing was to go 10 yards and stutter-step and sell him the

Preston Pearson (26) celebrates on the sideline in the December 1979 win over Washington.

inside move by turning my shoulders and my head as though I was looking back at the quarterback. Once he saw that, he bit. After that it was a footrace. Staubach threw it out in front just enough, and I dived to make sure I had it, so that when I fell it was in my arms. Of course I fell on the ball and I couldn't breathe, but he threw it perfectly, and it was a touchdown. Because of that, going into the locker room we felt so much better about ourselves, and you could see a little bit of deflation on the other side. And you could feel it."

And it carried over to the start of the third quarter. The Redskins took the kickoff and made one first down, but Harvey Martin sacked Theismann on the next play, and Washington punted. From 52 yards away it took Staubach just eight plays to get to the 2, and Newhouse redeemed his earlier fumble with a touchdown run over right guard. From a 17–0 deficit in the second quarter, the Cowboys had come all the way back to lead 21–17.

And the fun was just beginning.

Another exchange of punts, and the Redskins started at their 13. They were also not done for the day. Hall of Fame running back John Riggins ran for 5, 7, 10 and 4 yards. Two passes to John McDaniel, a Theismann scramble, and the possession had now lapped over into the fourth quarter. A procedure penalty slowed the drive and forced Washington to settle for a field goal: 21–20 Dallas, 11:24 left to play.

And now the Redskins defense rose to the occasion. The Cowboys started at their 14, and on the third play, Murphy intercepted Staubach's pass at the 25. Cliff Harris was called for interference in the end zone, and Riggins slammed in for the score. All that work, and now Washington had the lead back 27–21.

But wait, there's more.

Dallas goes three and out. From his own 34 Riggins

*Tony Hill catches
the winning pass
against the
Redskins in
December 1979.*

gallops around the right end, right past the Cowboys' bench, 66 yards for a backbreaking touchdown. Six minutes, fifty-four seconds left, and the Redskins lead the biggest game of the year, 34–21.

But with nearly seven minutes to go, there was still too much time left for the Cowboys to make a move. Apparently, they wanted a lot of people listening to Charlie and me on the radio. They went three and out again, and when they went out, so did more than half the capacity Texas Stadium crowd.

"When we finally got the lead, we thought we were on a roll," Staubach recalls. "But they scored seventeen straight points after that." And what was Staubach, Captain Comeback, thinking after Riggins broke the long run?

"Well, I'm trying to not ever get negative, but it didn't look good," he admits. (I hope Charlie Waters reads this. When the Cowboys mounted their eventual heart-stopping comeback, I chided the fans who had left. "Shame on you folks for leaving early." "No, Brad, shame on *you*," Waters shouted in glee. "You've got to *love* the Dallas Cowboys! They're the most exciting team in the NFL! And shame on you, lowly announcer, for not believing!" At least now I know even Staubach had his doubts.)

"When I saw on the films later, all the Redskins jumping on the sidelines and hugging each other [and then we won]. That was great," Staubach smiles. "But at the time, and after that interception I threw, that's when it looked bad. It looked like they had put it away. I don't mean I was a quarterback on the sidelines thinking the game was put away, but your emotions are affected by that, yeah."

So Washington took over with a thirteen-point lead at the Dallas 48 and just 5:21 to play. All they had to do was hold on to the ball, and . . .

Fumble!

On third down and four, Clarence Harmon dropped the ball and Randy White jumped on it for the Cowboys.

Staubach knew he didn't have Drew Pearson, who really couldn't run on that bad knee. "So I started talking to Tony Hill about the things he could do, because I needed to rely on somebody. He and Preston made some big catches."

With 3:49 to play, down 34–21, Dallas found itself at its 41 yard line. "We knew what they were doing," Staubach says. "They had started to play some zone, and we were able to find people open in the middle of it."

In just three plays: 14 to Butch Johnson, 19 to Hill, 26 for a touchdown to Ron Springs, it was Washington 34, Dallas 28, with 2:20 left in the game. "That was one of the best drives ever," Staubach says, "because that gave us hope. I knew once we scored that if we got the ball back, we had a real good shot at winning, because we had them figured out a little bit. But I didn't know if we'd get the ball back."

Which brings us to perhaps my favorite play in twenty-four years of Cowboys games.

The Redskins took the kickoff at their 25. All they needed was a first down. On second and 10, Riggins ran for 8. He had

For a Song

Redskins owner George Preston Marshall was blocking the vote to approve the Cowboys' entry into the NFL in 1960 until Cowboys owner Clint Murchison purchased the copyright to the Washington theme song, "Hail to the Redskins," and refused to let the Redskins play it until they voted Dallas into the league.

now rushed for 153 yards and two touchdowns. Everyone in the park knew where the ball was going . . . including venerable defensive tackle Larry Cole.

Now in his twelfth season, Cole was not the most famous Dallas defender. Not on a team with Harvey Martin, Randy White, John Dutton, and Cliff Harris. But none of them ever made a bigger play, which Cole, a successful home builder in Bedford, Texas, remembers and recounts as though he were narrating a replay.

"It was a toss sweep, which they'd run earlier. It was the center's job to cut me off at the tackle. You can't overcommit because the counter play was straight up the middle. I just felt that they would go this way instead, so at the snap of the ball, I just anticipated the sweep instead of the counter that came inside. I surprised myself how fast I got out there. I mean . . . that was John Riggins."

What would have happened had the Redskins run the counter? "There would have been a pretty big hole because my gap was really uncovered in that defense on that play," Cole says and chuckles. "Because they can't have a do-over.

"But by my twelfth year," he adds, "I wasn't guessing so much. I'm proud that in my professional career, I made the right judgment a lot. This wasn't luck. This was a skill, based on knowing how to play that play correctly. So I got to him and tackled him, and that was my job. But I felt like the whole crowd was tackling with me, because there was such an eruption on that play from the fans. I've never felt that kind of reaction."

Says Cliff Harris: "I could have kissed Larry at that moment."

But the work was not done, even after the Washington punt. "We could have stopped them, and if we'd gone three and out, no one would have remembered that play," Cole notes. "To do the script right, you've got to finish it off. Roger's made a big deal about it, but frankly, I think you've got to make a big deal out of Preston Pearson making those possession catches. Now that was something."

And now it's Washington 34, Dallas 28. The clock reads 1:46 left. Dallas, first and 10 at its own 25. Okay, Rog, your ball.

"They were playing the zone, and we started hitting the creases. Preston made a move on the linebacker and made a couple of big catches."

Larry Cole (63) tackles Washington's John Riggins (44) to set up the Cowboys' big 1979 win over the Redskins.

Preston Pearson: "On the last drive the crowd was going berserk, and that *did* give us some energy. You could feel it from head to toe. And I think the legacy of Staubach gives you that kind of gut feeling too. Now, we're thinking, aha, we've got Roger, plus a lot of other veteran guys in that huddle who had been in that situation before."

It's second and 10 at the Dallas 45, and Preston Pearson remembers Landry called for a "B-sideline curl. This goes back to a game against the Rams in '75, where Tom made an adjustment in the route during the game because of the way the Rams were playing me. Monte Coleman, Washington's linebacker, jammed me at the line of scrimmage and tried to push me toward the sideline, but because of that adjustment Tom made, Roger knew to look for me curling back." That pass went for 22 yards. Two plays later Staubach again went to Preston Pearson, this time for 25 yards. Forty-five seconds remained, and Dallas was first and goal on the 8.

On second and goal Landry and Staubach harkened back a month to the Redskins' win at RFK. "We had the same thing up there," says Staubach. "Landry liked to call this '13' pass to Billy Joe [DuPree, the tight end], but up there the Redskins blitzed us. If they blitzed again this time, we didn't have time for Billy Joe to run the options on the route, and I got sacked on it in D.C. Tom had a little tendency to repeat plays, and I would remember those. So because they blitzed in D.C., I knew they were going to blitz again, and I told Tony Hill as we broke the huddle, 'Make a move on [cornerback] Lemar Parish,' because Tony was not supposed to be a factor on the play at all. Parish was dogging him; Tony made his move, and Parish was toast on that deal. I just lobbed it to him."

The end result wasn't just a game observers remember. Says Larry Cole: "That was one of the most satisfying wins of my career. To me that was the epitome of the Cowboys, the peak of what we were and what we became. And as it turned out, it was the last of Roger's comebacks." Because of a series of concussions, Staubach retired, reluctantly, after the 1979 season.

And it's not his last game—a playoff loss to the Rams— that Staubach dwells on as a finale. It is this one. "I don't think I've ever been that excited."

I know just how you feel, Rog.

Ham 'n' Eggs

This is a story about two brothers. Two men born two months apart to different parents. Two men who didn't meet until months after their twenty-first birthdays. Two men thrown together by fate or circumstances in the spring of 1970, and who today, more than thirty-three years later, remain joined at the hip.

This is the story of Cliff and Charlie.

To Cowboys fans of almost any vintage, that's all you have to say: Cliff and Charlie. (For some reason it's almost never Charlie and Cliff.)

Cliff Harris and Charlie Waters are not related by blood. Charlie was born September 10, 1948, in North Augusta, South Carolina. Cliff came along almost exactly two months later, November 12, in Fayetteville, Arkansas. Charlie was a quarterback and wide receiver at Clemson University. Cliff was a defensive back at Ouachita Baptist University in Arkadelphia, Arkansas.

The Dallas Cowboys brought them together in the early spring of 1970. Charlie was a third-round draft choice that year. Cliff was signed as an undrafted free agent. They haven't been apart since, even when they were.

Like most teams the Cowboys through the years have had combinations of players who became linked in public perception. Sometimes it was because they played similar positions at the same time, like defensive ends Ed Jones and Harvey Martin. Sometimes it was because they complemented each other. It's hard to think of Roger Staubach without calling to mind Drew Pearson. It's impossible to recollect the three Super Bowl champions of the 1990s without envisioning "the Triplets": Troy Aikman, Emmitt Smith, and Michael Irvin.

But never have two or more players joined physically and emotionally, on the field and off, during their playing days and after, like Cliff and Charlie. In their prime, which was also one of the juiciest periods in Cowboys' history, they were Butch and Sundance. They went together like ham and eggs, peanut butter and jelly. Cliff and Charlie. And they still do.

In their first decade in the NFL, the 1960s, the Cowboys won one playoff game (not counting another win in the late and unlamented Playoff Bowl). It was probably coincidence that in Cliff and Charlie's rookie year, 1970, the Cowboys went to their first Super Bowl. In 1971 they won their first Super Bowl. They went to three more Super Bowls and won another NFL championship before Cliff retired after the 1979 season. (Ironically, that was a year Charlie missed with a preseason knee injury. He played two more campaigns before his retirement in 1981, but more on that later.)

Cliff Harris and Charlie Waters became "linked" in the 1970s because for most of the decade they were the Cowboys safeties. But it didn't start out that way. Originally, they were both cornerbacks. That didn't last long; coaches could tell quickly Cliff was a free safety. But the fact that they were penciled in for the same position is what first drew them together.

Today, partners in Energy Transfer Company in Dallas, they sit in a conference room and relive the beginnings of their lives together. They are a delight to watch and listen to. Like an old married couple, they finish each other's sentences and get sidetracked telling a story while they haggle over details.

"We immediately gravitated to each other," Waters remembers, "because we were in the same situation. This was after the draft in February, so it would have been a prerookie camp in March. I had been drafted and Cliff was a free agent, but I was a quarterback in college. I was totally lost coming in to learn about the secondary, so we fed off each other because I think we were both driven. We both knew the other one had a lot of competitive drive, and we just got along with each other."

In 1969 the Cowboys started Phil Clark and the great Cornell Green at the corners. The safeties were Mike Gaechter and future Hall of Famer Mel Renfro. So, as Waters recalls, "It was a turning point year for the Cowboys' veterans. At first we thought we could both make the team, but then it looked like we both might not make it."

Cliff interjects: "When we went into training camp and things began to settle as far as who might be doing what, Richmond Flowers, who was a second-year safety—and remember, as a second-year guy, he had a hundred percent more knowledge than us, he knew everything—he said, well, of the three of us, two would make it. He said one would make the starting lineup, one would play special teams, and one would be cut."

Charlie again: "And then right at the end of training camp they had a race. [Player-coach] Dan [Reeves] was always nice to me because we were from the same part of the country, and Dan called me one day and said, look, there's going to be a race this afternoon."

Cliff: "I didn't know that. I wish I had."

Charlie: "Cliff had shown up real well in all the preseason games. I said to Dan, 'Well, who's it between?' He said, 'You, Cliff, and Richmond.' Richmond was a track guy. We'd all played about the same amount in preseason, so we decided

Cliff Harris (right) and Charlie Waters in a light moment at training camp.

that the guy who won the race was going to make the team and the guy who comes in second will be on the taxi squad. The other one's gonna get cut." With a hearty laugh and the comfort of the intervening years, Waters flashes his still-boyish grin. "We looked around at each other and said, 'Well, see you later, Charlie.' I was the slowest of the three.

"So that afternoon we all raced, and I tell you what, it was as close to a dead heat as anything I've been in in my life. It kind of freaked me out that I kept up with them. Fear was a great motivator. And maybe it was because we all ran pretty fast, but we all made the team. Richmond eventually got gone, and Cliff and I stayed together for a long time."

But not yet as Butch and Sundance. Once the 1970 season began, they were both safeties, competing for a while for the same job. Or at least it appeared so. They never really took it that way.

"Although we were both competing at the same position," Charlie says, "we were two different kinds of ballplayers. Cliff played a little corner in preseason, but after a while it was clear he was a free safety. I played a little corner in preseason but I certainly wasn't a corner. I was playing strong safety."

The way it shook out by the time the Cowboys opened the 1970 season in Philadelphia, the starting corners were Renfro and former Green Bay Packers all-pro Herb Adderley. Cornell Green had moved to strong safety, and Cliff won the starting free safety job. "We knew there was competition between us," says Waters, "but we never felt that way. We both had a thirst for learning. I'd always go to Cliff with questions and he'd always come to me. And I always envisioned from the very get-go of someday us playing in the secondary together."

But not yet. At the beginning of the season, Harris was the starter. "Cliff clearly made a statement in the NFL by starting the first six games," Waters says. "I was a backup, and happy as a pig in slop that I'm a backup and Cliff's a star."

And then real life intervened.

Cliff Harris was in a National Guard unit in 1970, and in midseason—with war in Vietnam raging—his unit was called up. "While Cliff was on ready duty, someone had to play his position, and it was me," says Charlie. "Then on the weekends he had to come back and watch me play his position. It put a little strain on our relationship, but I think it helped build it more than anything. Then we got very competitive."

In this early stage of their relationship, Harris and Waters found themselves constantly striving to keep up with and outdo each other. It would be a competition they would carry on over the years, whether it was, as Harris notes, "football, racquetball, lifting weights, or racing dirt bikes."

Waters started the Super Bowl, and then the 1971 season. For a while. "Then they saw the light," he grins, "and put Cliff back in there. I moved back into a strong safety backup role. And from then on there was never any competition again between us in football. We just tried to learn from each other."

Never again a football competition, but always a drive to push each other, make each other better . . . and here Waters uses the "b" word: "like brothers."

"We kept on doing everything else against each other," Cliff remembers. "It's a similar trait you see in everyone successful in the NFL. You see it in every training camp. Guys compete against each other on the football field, and then they come back after beating up on each other all day and what do they do? They play cards. They play dominoes, they play darts—something that drives them from a competitive standpoint. We've done that naturally all these years, but for a while it was hard to distinguish one kind of competition from another."

But finally in 1971 Cliff and Charlie were not competing against each other for the same football job. Remember, both had envisioned from early on that they'd someday pair up. So was it a relief when they were no longer playing the same position? "We've never talked about that," says Charlie, "because it's just so damned serious. But I felt like all was right with the world, because I didn't feel like I was a better player than Cliff at the free safety position. As much as I wanted to play, Cliff was the free safety. Finally, we were playing the positions we should play."

Cliff Harris (center) and Charlie Waters (right) talk sideline strategy with teammate Mark Washington in their playing days.

"I think we were two different types of players," says Harris, touching now on the spark of what would be a decade of almost indescribable chemistry between them. "Charlie could play corner, but I think they saw him as a safety eventually. I think [Coach Tom] Landry saw some of himself in Charlie: limited physical ability as a corner, but enough to be effective playing within the Landry system."

In 1972 Waters was moved to corner, a position at which he would start in 1973 and 1974. By his own admission Waters struggled at the position. But "when I was at corner was when Cliff and I began to develop defenses that they still run today. We started creating schemes to somehow figure out a way to win."

"You've got to think about who was back there in the secondary," Cliff says, and Charlie chuckles at the memory. "Cornell Green was the strong safety, I was the free safety, Mel Renfro was one corner, and Charlie was the other corner. Now, where do you think they're throwing the ball?

"We played a lot of middle zone, and I would lean toward helping Charlie. It couldn't be a complete dominant thing, because Mel was a guy who would let you know if you weren't where you were supposed to be. He'd let you know what was coming ahead of time. But that's when Charlie and I started developing a rapport, a kind of mental telepathy, when he could expect to get help from me in standard defenses when normally he wouldn't get help. And it wasn't necessarily to help Charlie. It was because that was what gave us the best chance to win."

It wasn't until 1975 that Waters and Harris started at safety together—a year, not coincidentally, during which the Cowboys forged an unlikely trip to the Super Bowl as a wild card, with the "Dirty Dozen" rookies who made the team. Quite a class that was. The draftees included Randy White, Thomas Henderson, Bob Breunig, Pat Donovan, Randy Hughes, Mike Hegman, Herb Scott, and Scott Laidlaw. All of that talent, plus the experience that Waters and Harris had gained playing together since Waters moved into the lineup at corner in 1973, was a big factor in the Cowboys' success.

Money Time

Charlie Waters is the Cowboys' career playoff interception leader with nine in twenty-five playoff games. His forty-one career regular-season interceptions (the same as his jersey number) rank third on the team's all-time list.

"We always liked to say that we created an extra person on the field," recalls Waters. "It was like there was an extra guy out there, a third safety. Because as weird as it sounds, we talked about one fist of steel and another of iron. All the techniques we used at corner, we incorporated in the safety position. I looked to Cliff to teach me how to tackle and to hit, and he looked to me to try to steal the ball a little bit more. I'd say, 'You need to get the ball instead of hitting the guy in the mouth.' And he'd say, 'Well, you need to hit the guy in the mouth once in a while instead of going for the ball.' Whatever he didn't do, I did. And whatever I didn't do, he did. Whether it was one of us taking a certain angle and the other taking a different one, or a certain velocity involved, we covered each other. Every player has a strength and a weakness, but there were no weaknesses with us because we covered each other."

Cliff Harris (43) brings down Buffalo's O. J. Simpson. As usual, Charlie Waters (41) is close at hand.

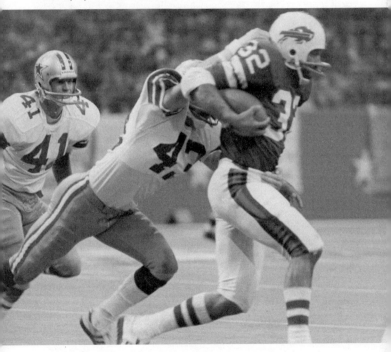

But don't believe them, listen to Gene Stallings, who became the Cowboys' secondary coach in 1972. He was in charge for the entire tenure of Cliff and Charlie.

"Best pair of safeties I ever saw," Stallings says with no hesitation from his home in Paris, Texas, where he lives in alleged retirement.

Ever?

"Ever. 'Course, I only coached in the league eighteen years. Charlie was smart, a student of the game. Cliff was aggressive, just an intimidating hitter. They were the perfect complement to each other. Each by himself was very good. Together, they were the best."

Cliff and Charlie are writing their own book about their years together. (Cliff says he wants the title to be, *It's Only a Game, but Don't Tell Coach Landry*.) In it, Charlie says they'll tell countless stories of times in games when they just looked at each other and freelanced a defensive wrinkle. Then he shares one.

As Waters diagrams a defense they changed with an ad lib, Harris says, "It's stimulating just talking about the synergy we've always had. It demonstrates how we were able to be more effective by using each other's strengths and weaknesses, and that was by disguising what we were going to do. I think a critical component of pass defense is the confusion of the quarterback. For a period of time, he's not gonna know what's happening out there."

Charlie: "Landry taught us to think that way. It was part of our philosophy."

Cliff: "And the sooner the guy knows, the faster he can read it, the more in danger you are of getting beat. That's where Charlie and I worked so well, and confusing the quarterbacks is what leads to traps." (He means "sacks," but Coach Landry referred to them as "traps.")

Now Charlie diagrams the Cowboys' "special" defense, used in a certain game in Philadelphia in 1975. "See, Cliff's free and I'm in this area here. The tight end goes down and breaks out to the right, and the back slides out underneath him. The first time they run this play, I cover the tight end and they throw to the back and complete it for about 7 yards. Now it's like seven plays later in the series, and we haven't had a chance to go to the bench and change the defense. So they come out in the same formation, and Cliff and I just look at each other. So I go cover the back, because I knew where they threw it last time and the quarterback knows that I know it; so I go to the back, knowing he'll throw to the

Good Value

Cliff Harris (six appearances) is one of ten Cowboys who were undrafted free agents out of college to play in the Pro Bowl. The others follow:

Cornerback Don Bishop (1962)
Defensive back Cornell Green (1965–67, 1971–72)
Center Dave Manders (1966)
Wide receiver Drew Pearson (1974, 1976–77)
Cornerback Everson Walls (1981–83)
Special teams Bill Bates (1984)
Offensive guard Nate Newton (1992–96, 1998)
Offensive tackle Mark Tuinei (1994–95)
Special teams Jim Schwantz (1996)

open tight end. Except he's not open, because Cliff cuts in front of him and makes the interception. We didn't tell anyone else. We couldn't. No one else would understand it. We just did it."

Cliff and Charlie swear they did this as a common practice the next three years. Stallings isn't so sure. "Look, I broke down every film. That just couldn't happen that much, because it was Coach Landry's defense. It was coordinated with the fronts. I think through the years myth can become a little bigger than what happened. I know they like to talk about all that, but I saw every film. I'd know." (And then you look at Cliff and Charlie, and you're mindful of two brothers sneaking out the upstairs window and going out and raising hell and coming back before anyone knew, and their dad says, no, not *my* boys. I'd know.)

Cliff and Charlie were famous among their teammates for having heated arguments on the field, during games, about what defenses to run. Did their improvisation ever backfire?

"Do you remember the Super Bowl in Miami?" Charlie says, meaning Super Bowl XIII, which the Cowboys lost to Pittsburgh 35–31. Cliff starts shaking his head and cursing Terry Bradshaw under his breath as Charlie resumes furiously diagramming plays.

Cliff can't contain himself, though, leaning over Charlie's shoulder and pointing to the diagram. "We're in a '33' defense, which is based on the tight end. If he runs an outside route, Charlie takes him and I cover for him. If he runs an inside route, I take him and Charlie covers for me. At one point, in a certain formation, I said to Charlie, 'Let's switch roles. I'll run over and cover the wide receiver, and he'll think it's our '34' defense, and we'll play each other's roles. But it looks like something else. Bradshaw will think Charlie's isolated on the tight end, and if he runs this inside route, Charlie will have trouble covering him. Except I'll tear ass back and get to the middle and intercept the ball."

So let me guess? You come running back to the middle and Bradshaw hits an open Lynn Swann?

"Worse," says Charlie. "We designed this for Jim Hart and the Cardinals. It worked on them, because Hart's a smart quarterback and he'll do what the defense tells him. It didn't work on that dumbass Bradshaw. He's got to throw to the tight end, because he's open, except with our little wrinkle he wasn't. So what does he do? He hands it off to Franco [Harris], I run into the umpire, and Franco runs clean up the middle for a touchdown. The next day in the paper we read where Bradshaw said, 'I saw Cliff move out and I knew it was a blitz, so I audibled to a trap.' A *blitz*! It wasn't a blitz, and it's not even a good call against a blitz! We just looked each other and said, 'Well, [bleep] me standing up.' "

In 1979 Charlie tore up his knee in a preseason game in Seattle and missed the whole year. Cliff played alongside Randy Hughes, a fine player, but not Charlie. What was that like for him?

"If you go on vacation to the Cayman Islands by yourself, it's not a lot of fun. If you go with a buddy you can hang out with, that's fun. That's what makes football enjoyable. When Charlie left, it became more of a job. Other guys didn't know the defenses, and normally they'd look to Charlie. Without him there was no creativity. Take the creativity out of life, and you're not going to have the passion."

Cliff also accumulated injuries in 1979, including a dangerous one to his neck, so he retired after the season. Charlie tried to talk him out of it, but to no avail, and he was left without Cliff for his last two years.

Charlie Waters (left) and Cliff Harris at a Cowboys' reunion in the 1990s.

"There was a big void," he remembers. "We had a bunch of rookies in the secondary, and they called us 'Charlie's Angels.' But it didn't fill the void. I had to grow up and realize that what I had with Cliff back there, I wasn't going to have any more. It was fine as far as it went, but it wasn't like Cliff and I playing touch football on Sunday afternoon."

Cliff went into business. Charlie went into broadcasting, then coaching, and finally moved back to Dallas a few years ago and went back into business with Cliff. But even when they were apart, they weren't.

Charlie's youngest son, who was born on November 12, is named Cliff. Why did Cliff not reciprocate? "You'll have to ask my ex-wife," he shrugs.

Actually, Charlie says naming his son Cliff was his wife Rosie's idea. " 'They have the same birthday' she said. 'You *have* to name him Cliff.' "

"Yeah," Cliff says with a chuckle. "And now every time she sees me, she says 'Damn, Cliff, he acts just like you.' "

Booms and Busts

NFL head coaches think they have difficult jobs.

Oh, sure, they have to make split-second decisions in front of thousands of screaming people every week. During the season they seldom sleep or see their families. Movies, books, TV? Please. And when the season's over, they have days on end to unwind before starting the whole process over.

But how tough can it be when you have so much help? There are hundreds of thousands of volunteer experts offering their assistance on call-in shows, Internet sites, and in letters to the editor. Think about it. You have to do your job by yourself. Coaches are never alone.

In fact there's probably only one individual on a football team who has it easier than the head coach.

That would be the general manager.

When the coach is hiring a staff, he doesn't have all those amateur assistants telling him who should be hired as the defensive line coach, or for special teams or tight ends. But the GM, he's got all those volunteers and their cousins offering aid when it's time to hire a coach. Sometimes they even tell him when that time is. And the GM doesn't have to answer to himself about the decision to kick or go for it.

So with all that help, why can't these guys draft?

In no other sport is the draft of college talent as critical to replenishing the player supply. Basketball only has a two-round draft, and the second round doesn't count any more. Hockey and baseball have minor-league systems to season their talent, and they can emulate soccer and go overseas for key players about whom the public may never have heard.

Not football. In the NFL your draft is everything, and with the advent of the strictest salary cap in professional athletics, it's become more important than ever. You can sign a veteran free agent but that costs. Because of the cap trades for players have become almost as rare as a dropkick (you're showing your age if you got that reference). And not only do you have to draft the right players, they have to be able to play and produce right away. There are very few teams that can afford the luxury of a development project any more.

Drafting has always been an inexact science, and with the media explosion of the last few years creating as many sideline experts in April as there are in October, it's become even more stressful. People armed with lots of hair spray go on national television as soon as a pick is made to proclaim to the world its wisdom or folly.

Still, every good fan loves to debate the merits of what his or her favorite team has done in the draft. Dallas fans are certainly no exception, and they've frequently had plenty to talk about. The 2002 draft that brought safety Roy Williams, guard-center Andre Gurode, receiver Antonio Bryant, corner-back Derek Ross, and fullback Jamar Martin looks like the team's most successful in many, many years. Recent history has been (ahem) somewhat less kind on draft day.

When the Cowboys came into the league in 1960, scouting bore little resemblance to what it's since become. Late in that decade some teams were still bringing a copy of Street and Smith's scouting magazine to the draft room for last-minute help. Dallas got in on the cutting edge of modern scouting under Gil Brandt, who helped introduce the use of computers and other sophisticated scouting tools, and for a long time, they were way ahead of the curve. It seemed they were always simply plugging in a Randy White to replace a Bob Lilly. It didn't always work quite that way, but it seemed to.

Then, gradually, other teams began to catch up. Everyone got computerized. The Cowboys had a stretch of years where they had better teams, so they drafted lower (or higher, depending on your point of view), and years of drafting in the twenties yielded fewer premium results. That led to taking a few gambles, and when some of those turned out to be dry holes, the magic began to erode.

Larry Lacewell is the Cowboys' director of college and pro scouting. He's been with the team since 1992, and since 1993 he's helped owner–general Manager Jerry Jones direct the draft. Lacewell's advice is that before you start evaluating draft results, you ought to first establish your parameters.

"It's a crapshoot," he says for openers. "What you try to do is you set a certain standard, certain measurables, certain traits

Scouting director Larry Lacewell (right, with 2002 first round pick Roy Williams) has helped run the Cowboys' draft preparations since 1993.

that you look for in individuals, and you stick with them. If they don't have those, then you try to move on. It might be speed, it might be character, it might be size. For example, in the Landry days, they almost had a cookie cutter. If the guy didn't look *that way*, they weren't taking him. If it was a 5'11" linebacker, they weren't taking him. He played the percentages of what the NFL looks like. Well, over the years there's been a changing face in the league. The game has changed to the point where you just can't stamp the cookie cutter. Speed has become more prevalent at all positions. Sometimes you have to give up size to get it. Everybody in the world wants a big, fast guy. We all want that. Big, fast, tough, and smart. But then if he doesn't have all those ingredients, tell me about some other ingredients."

Jerry Jones has tried to apply a scientific method to formulate his draft philosophy. "There needs to be a recognition," he says, "that if you look at the top ten picks [overall in each draft] in the last fourteen years, half of them would be considered busts, were not acceptable. On the other hand the best chance to get a premier player is in the top five picks. Those dynamics strike at you, that if you're not up in that top five, you need to expect you could be wrong half the time."

In order to reduce those odds, Jones has tried to do the math. Former Cowboys executive Mike McCoy, who was part of the front-office team in the first few years after Jones bought the team, came up with a formula based on past drafts. "In 1989," Jones recalls, "he quantified trades that were made for draft picks. He put a numerical evaluation, a number of points, on every pick in the draft, from the first one all the way down through the last pick in the seventh round. That gave you an idea where if you had the fifteenth pick in the draft, and someone called and said, 'We want to trade you our pick, which is at the bottom of the round, plus our number three,' then you can add them up and see who's getting the better of the deal. This is a formula that is now commonly used all over the NFL."

There are exceptions to the formula, so that a team doesn't become a prisoner of its research. According to Jones: "The thing that has to be factored in is if there's a player there where your evaluation of his talent would make you say, 'Even if the numbers are pretty close, I'd rather have the player.'"

The formula also supports what seems to be basic logic: The more picks you have, the better chance you have of finding good players, plural. That's why Jones has frequently been willing to trade down in the first round. And there's another reason, one brought on by the demands of the salary cap. "Starting with the cap era," Jones explains, "it was very important to us to use our dollars to keep our veteran players, rather than to draft a player where we questioned his ability to come in and start for us. The bottom line is between 1989 and 1994 we had something like 8 or 9,000 points to draft with. The only other clubs who have ever had those kinds of points to draft with have been expansion clubs. We got those points not only by having high picks that we earned with poor records in 1988 and '89, but also from the extra draft choices we got in the Herschel Walker trade (with Minnesota in the fall of 1989). So during that four- or five-year period, we had like three and a half to four times the amount of points than if you add up all of our years since."

So that's the approach. But the human element still comes into play in the persons of drafters and players. If there were no judgments to make, every pick would work out in the first half of the draft, and every team would finish 8–8. There are variables to be considered, and one of them is the position your man plays.

Here's an example: It would be difficult to find a better draft choice in Cowboys history than Troy Aikman—franchise quarterback who's going to the Hall of Fame, won three Super Bowls, broke all Cowboys' passing records, and was a leader and the poster boy for work ethic. You got all kinds of value for that pick. But on the other hand, he was the first overall pick. Isn't that guy supposed to be a superstar? I mean, come on. I could have drafted Troy Aikman. That didn't take any drafting talent, did it?

Well, maybe. It's almost impossible to remember now, but leading up to draft day in 1989, there was more than a little debate, both inside the organization and around the NFL, about whether the right pick was Aikman or Michigan State's All-American offensive tackle, Tony Mandarich.

Because the Cowboys had the first overall pick, they had the right to sign their player before the draft, and they had signed Aikman on Thursday. On Friday, April 21, *USA Today* columnist Rudy Martzke quoted ESPN draft analyst Joe Theismann as saying, "They're taking Aikman to sell tickets. . . . The Cowboys have done everything in their power to embarrass the greatest NFL franchise in the past thirty years." Jerry Jones cackles about the blurb. "I send that to Joe every five years or so," he laughs. But that wasn't all. ESPN's top draftnik, Mel Kiper, told Martzke in the same article that the Cowboys' NFC East opponents "hoped the Cowboys would take Aikman. If they took Tony Mandarich, he'd give Dallas a virtual 300-pound [per man] line for Herschel Walker to run behind." Walker, of course, was traded to Minnesota that October. Mandarich was taken second overall by Green Bay, played six injury-plagued seasons stretched over nine years with two teams, and made virtually no impact.

That, according to Larry Lacewell, is where you have to

Top Cats

The Cowboys have had the number one overall pick in the draft three times. All three (Ed Jones in 1974, Troy Aikman in 1989, and Russell Maryland in 1991) became Pro Bowl players.

put a caveat on evaluating a top pick: "If you screw a number one [overall] draft choice up at quarterback, your franchise might not get over that for a long time. You've taken the number one person in the whole draft and said, 'This is our quarterback of the future.' If you screw that up, it's as costly as it can get." And apparently, because of the importance of the position, any high first-round pick of a quarterback renders the drafter sleepless until the player proves he's not, with apologies, Akili Smith or Ryan Leaf.

If you've ever followed a team or a draft, you must have wanted at some juncture to ask someone in authority how it happens that some picks flop so grandly. No one sets out to draft poorly, after all. Larry Lacewell? "I don't think any of us still know. We look at the quarterback position and scratch our heads. I think Norv Turner [the former Cowboys offensive coordinator now with the Miami Dolphins] knows a quarterback, but yet he took Heath Shuler [when Turner was head coach of the Washington Redskins]. He had a quarterback in [Trent] Green and traded him away. Now Trent Green's still playing and making a lot of money [in Kansas City] and Shuler's out of the league. So for me to tell you somebody has that answer, I can't do that. If someone could tell you why all the busts happen, then maybe we wouldn't repeat ourselves."

What a great answer. Demosthenes, meet Larry Lacewell.

A good pick would seem to be a player taken in a late round who winds up being a star. An example might be Leon

Lett, the big defensive tackle taken in the seventh round in 1991 from tiny Emporia State. Lett gave the Cowboys ten solid years and went to two Pro Bowls before running into off-field problems. That's amazing production from a seventh-round pick. But sometimes you have to be lucky. As Lacewell admits, "If we knew Leon Lett was that good, we wouldn't have tried to be that smart and wait till the seventh round."

So admitting that there's a lot of luck involved, and that sometimes teams outsmart themselves, we humbly offer one subjective list of some of the best and a few of the worst draft choices in Cowboys history. Your list may differ. There's no right or wrong answer, and that's the fun of it. The only qualification is that a pick that's supposed to be good and turns out that way won't be on this list. Sorry, Troy, I still think I could have drafted you.

This list will not be in any particular order, except for what we offer as the best pick in the history of the franchise: offensive lineman Larry Allen in the second round, the forty-sixth player selected, in 1994. Was Allen a better football player than Aikman, Roger Staubach, Emmitt Smith, Bob Lilly? Who knows? How can you tell? But to date, Allen has been selected to seven Pro Bowls, more than any Cowboys offensive lineman ever. He was on the 1990s all-decade team and is a cinch Hall of Famer. My choice is (somehow not surprisingly) supported by the men who drafted him.

Says Lacewell: "There was a period where he was *the* best lineman in the NFL. You just couldn't believe he was that good. That's why he went in the second round. Now, if he'd done what we saw on film at Ohio State instead of Sonoma, he'd have been a first-rounder. You just had to pinch yourself. We had him listed in our first round, and when he fell out, [scout] Tom Ciscowski, [offensive line coach] Hudson Houck, and I ran into the office next door and put his tape back on to make sure what we'd seen was really there. Maybe we were dreaming. We tried every way in the world to talk ourselves out of it. When you think a guy is great and no one else does, you begin to second-guess yourself. Maybe one reason he fell is that as I understand it he had a terrible workout [for pro scouts before the draft]. But we didn't go. Thank God."

Somewhere behind Allen, I'll take four linemen from the Landry era. Before Larry Allen, the best offensive lineman in the history of the franchise was probably Rayfield Wright, the original "Big Cat." Dallas got him in the seventh round of a seventeen-round draft in 1967. He'd been a defensive end at Fort Valley State, and they originally brought him in to be a

Larry Allen (73) may have been the Cowboys' best-ever draft pick.

tight end. He was the full-time starting right tackle by his fourth season, played thirteen years, and was chosen for six Pro Bowls.

Larry Cole is high on my list. "Bubba," from Hawaii, was chosen after 427 other players, in the sixteenth round in 1968. He played thirteen years, returned three interceptions for touchdowns, and made some of the biggest plays in the history of the franchise. Not bad for a sixteenth-rounder. Cole was never a Pro Bowl player, but during his tenure four other defensive linemen were: Lilly, White, George Andrie, and Harvey Martin. Plus, Cole was in the Zero Club.

The same criteria put Jethro Pugh on the list. "Buzz" was an eleventh-round pick in 1965 from Elizabeth City State. (One of Gil Brandt's hallmarks was finding players from obscure schools.) Pugh played fourteen seasons and was one of the defensive anchors of five Super Bowl teams.

In 1975 the Cowboys were a surprise Super Bowl team based in large measure on the contributions of the "Dirty Dozen," twelve drafted players who made the team out of the nineteen who were drafted. On sheer numbers that may have been the best draft class in team history. It was led at the top by Randy White. Much more overlooked on draft day was the eleventh of the dozen, drafted player number 330: guard Herb Scott from Virginia Union. Herbie was a thirteenth-round pick who played ten years and went to three Pro Bowls.

That same class, by the way, produced Thomas Henderson, a pretty good first-round pick considering he came from Langston College. Brandt knew something. He could not have predicted Henderson's tragic battle with drugs that short-circuited his career, but that was a pretty gutsy pick that certainly worked out.

Loathe as we are to speak ill of people who do something we can't, we promised booms and busts, and goodness knows, there have been some busts. A bad pick is easier to choose: someone drafted high who performed low.

If you are a Cowboys fan of the last fifteen years, you may say Shante Carver, the 1994 first-rounder taken twenty-three selections ahead of Larry Allen. Clearly he underachieved, but was Carver a bust or did the Cowboys just take him too high? Says Lacewell: "We let ourselves get talked into taking a defensive end no matter what. Had we taken him in the third round, I'm not sure his career wouldn't have been much different. The expectations [of being a first-rounder] become so high on guys, it's unfair. You can't go into the room with the press and say, 'Y' know, we drafted this guy 'cause we needed an end, he's the sixth one taken and we were afraid if we didn't take him we weren't gonna get one.' You can't say it, but we've also learned a lesson here that it's a mistake to do it."

Perhaps you'd nominate Sherman Williams, a second round pick (and the Cowboys' first choice) in 1995. The Cowboys didn't like anyone with their twenty-eighth pick in the first round, so they traded out of the round and took Williams because they needed a backup ballcarrier. "That," says Lacewell, "was getting too cute." What made it worse was the player Tampa Bay took with that twenty-eighth pick: linebacker Derrick Brooks, who in 2002 was chosen for his sixth Pro Bowl.

Aiming High

The Cowboys' first pick in the draft has been a quarterback four times. Two were first-rounders: Aikman (number 1 overall in '89) and Craig Morton (number 6 overall in '65). Twice the Cowboys' first choice was used on a quarterback in the second round: Sonny Gibbs in '62 and Quincy Carter in 2001.

Rod Hill is our nominee for the Cowboys' worst-ever draft choice.

There are some doozies on this list. Bill Thomas, a running back picked with the last selection in the first round in 1972, was cut after one year. Kevin Brooks was a defensive end drafted with the seventeenth overall pick in 1985. This guy had an unbelievable physique. The problem was that he looked like Tarzan and played like Jane. He lasted four years in Dallas and two more in Detroit. And then there's Rod Hill.

Hill, my pick for the worst draft choice I've seen in twenty-five years, was the Cowboys' first pick in 1982. A cornerback from Kentucky State, Hill lasted six years in the league, but only two in Dallas. He was drafted partly for his speed on kick returns, but no one foresaw his penchant for running from sideline to sideline to avoid contact. His attitude was so bad that he was called out by teammates for not caring enough. And the worst part was the attitude Brandt displayed on draft day. Hoping to reproduce his small-college success one more time, Brandt came prancing out of the draft room waving a folded piece of white paper, proclaiming, "I've had our pick's name written down here for two weeks!"

That part wasn't Rod Hill's fault, but we'll blame him for the next two years.

Move Over, Sweetness

First things first: On the play on which Emmitt Smith became the all-time leading rusher in the history of the National Football League, he was so excited, he almost tripped over his own feet.

Or, to be more precise, he *did* trip. He almost fell down.

On a gray, drizzly winter's day, the holder of the most prestigious individual record in professional football sits in the richly but tastefully appointed study of his north Dallas home, wearing black sweat pants and a gray T-shirt. As he discusses the most memorable day of his professional life, he also wears a dazzling grin.

On the carry that put him in the record books, Emmitt Smith needed 9 yards to surpass the late Walter Payton's career mark of 16,726.

He had just picked up 3 yards, and the Cowboys were second and 7 at their 30 yard line against the Seattle Seahawks. Smith already had three carries for double-digit gains in the game. On the historic play fullback Robert Thomas pulled through the left guard-tackle gap and picked off strong safety Reggie Tongue. Left guard Jeremy McKinney walled off defensive tackle Chad Eaton. This was the hole Emmitt saw.

As he slipped through the crease, as he had done literally thousands of times before, Smith read his blockers. He was bumped, stumbled, and finally had to put his free hand on the ground to maintain his balance. Eleven yards later, before being tackled by free safety Ken Lucas, Emmitt Smith delivered the moment 65,000 people had come to see.

It wasn't clean. On FOX-TV, Pat Summerall's play-by-play call was that Smith "almost broke it," meaning a long gain for a touchdown. My radio call had two long pauses, one as I reported, "Smith to the 40 yard line." I had to hesitate because he was starting to pinball off people. Then, "Right on the mark. That should do it!"

Emmitt Smith remembers all of this months later as though he were watching it live, but now he can laugh. And he does, enthusiastically.

Reminded that he just barely got the yards he needed, Emmitt cackles, "If I hadn't been running so hard, I'd have gotten 60! If I hadn't been tripping and stumbling on my feet, I'd have probably scored a touchdown. I always said my perfect play for that run would have been a long touchdown. And that was it! That would have been a touchdown run. If I hadn't been stumbling over my own feet, I'd have cut back behind Ol' Boy [I think he means Thomas], and I'd have been off and running. [Cornerback] Shawn Springs would have had to come catch me with [wide receiver] Joey Galloway running with him, and I don't think that would have happened. Joey would have outrun him.

"I really started stumbling because I couldn't believe it. The hole opened up so big, and I was trying to hit it so hard to blow it wide open, that . . . I tripped!" Emmitt's eyes get big again, as though he is seeing it for the first time. But now he can chuckle, and shake his head, and know that that record is his, and no one can take it away from him. Until, of course, someone does.

Emmitt Smith bounces off the turf for the yards he needed to break Walter Payton's rushing record. It happened on this play!

Becoming professional football's all-time rushing leader was something a young Emmitt Smith had the audacity to write down and set as a goal when he was a rookie in 1990. He has said he did that because his high school coach taught him that dreams are only dreams until you write them down, and then they become goals.

But now he's willing to admit that when he wrote that down thirteen years before, the goal was still more of a dream. It didn't become a real goal until later. Possibly later than you think.

There's a difference between writing down a lofty goal as a wide-eyed rookie and realizing that it is truly within your grasp. When did that moment come for Smith?

"I think it came to a realization at the beginning of last year," he muses, and he means going into the 2002 season, when the cold, hard statistics showed he needed 540 yards to claim the record as his own. "Until then, it was still just words. The reason I say that is because I'm in the most demanding sport in America. I'm a realist. I know that to get there, I've got to go through certain things. I've got to go through game one through game sixteen, and I've got to stay healthy. If I'm healthy, I think I can get it done. So at the beginning of the 2002 season, when I saw I was at 540, I said, 'Okay. This can come down this year. And it *will* come down this year. But the thing that I need to do now is to not only perform, but I've got to stay healthy. That's the one variable you've got no control over. Outside of that, you can control how you train during the off-season, you can control how you approach the game, you can control your attitude, how you're studying, all of that.

"I also couldn't control what offense we were going to run. I didn't even know what offense we were going to run, or who would be blocking. So how could I say it was automatic? But I believed we could get it done. Although," and now he can laugh a little, "after that first game down in Houston, I thought, man, it's gonna be a long season if we can't beat these jokers here." (The Cowboys had begun the 2002 season losing to the Texans, becoming just the second team in NFL history to lose to an expansion team in its inaugural game.)

Being so close to a record he cherished so much did not change the way Emmitt Smith approached his job. He'd been through injuries before. There was the now famous separated shoulder he suffered in the season-ending win over the Giants in New York in 1993. His 1997 season was slowed by what surgery later showed to be bone spurs in his ankle, although he still finished with 1,074 yards that year. But he made few conscious concessions to age and the risk of injury.

"No, it didn't change anything about the way I approached each game," he says. "I'd still sell out my body. Maybe now I have to pick and choose a little more *when* I'm going to sell it out. There was a time I didn't pick and choose, but as I've gotten older, you have to know when to sell your body out. I mean *out* out. The importance of the game has something to do with that. I mean, they're all important, but some games are just a little more important than others."

From a team standpoint the Cowboys' meeting with Seattle on October 27, 2002, was not one of those games. The Cowboys entered the season with high hopes, but a rash of training camp injuries to the offensive line triggered wild inconsistency from the offense in general. Before the season many commentators and writers tried to predict when Payton's record would fall. Most guesses were either October 13, at home against Carolina, or the following week in Arizona. Shortly before that period, the Cowboys' offense started springing enough leaks to sink a battleship. They had lost that game in Arizona in overtime, a depressing 9–6 stinker in which Emmitt had gained 82 yards on twenty-two carries.

So they came to work on October 27 with a 3–4 record, facing a struggling Seahawks team. And the pressure was on. The Cowboys desperately wanted Emmitt to break the record at home. His pursuit of Payton, the man known as "Sweetness," was so central to the promotion of the team that a different picture of Smith adorned each game's tickets. But this Sunday before Halloween would be the club's last home game until the Sunday before Thanksgiving. There were two road games and a bye week in between. Emmitt also dearly wanted to break the record in front of Cowboys fans. (No one wanted it to happen the next week, in Detroit, where fans believed the record might have been Barry Sanders's had he not abruptly retired from the game two years before.)

Century Runners

Emmitt Smith is one of only three men in NFL history to rush for more than 100 yards in two different Super Bowls (108 versus Buffalo in XXVII, 132 versus Buffalo in XXVIII). Miami's Larry Csonka rumbled for 112 versus Washington in Super Bowl VII and 145 versus Minnesota in VIII. Denver's Terrell Davis punished Green Bay for 157 yards in Super Bowl XXXII and Atlanta for 102 in XXXIII.

But the lackluster performance of the team didn't matter on this particular day. Emmitt Smith was close to the record. Not just the record, but The Record. One can argue, and I will, that the only individual mark in American team sport more prestigious is baseball's career home run record. But he was still far enough away that he'd have to work for it. Rushing for 93 yards given the state of the Dallas offensive line seemed a daunting task. And if that weren't enough, the Cowboys chose the Seattle game to make a quarterback change.

Quincy Carter, the incumbent starter, had thrown four interceptions, two of them in the end zone, in the loss to the Cardinals. On Monday Coach Dave Campo and General Manager Jerry Jones announced a switch to backup Chad Hutchinson. This was fine, except that Hutchinson was making a return to football after four years away from the sport pitching for the St. Louis Cardinals, mostly in the minor leagues. He was making his NFL debut behind an offensive line for which patchwork would have been a promotion, in the game where Emmitt Smith needed 93 yards to become the game's all-time leading rusher.

October 27 in Dallas was a typical late-October day for north central Texas: sixty degrees, a little humid, a little cloudy, almost no wind. It felt like a good day to play football, a great day to break a record. As he has been most of his life when something important is at stake, Emmitt Smith was geeked. (Older readers may prefer "ready" or "equal to the task," but "ready" doesn't begin to describe Smith this day. He was in some stratosphere beyond "ready.")

As he recalls coming out of the Texas Stadium tunnel for warm-ups, "I can't say it was an experience to the level of a Super Bowl, because it was hard for me to separate [what I was trying to do] from the team. But it was a playoff atmosphere that I'll never forget. The air was full of excitement and joy. There was a sweet aroma about being there, like something spectacular will be happening today. To know that it was here in Texas Stadium was an amazing, amazing moment. There's never been a Super Bowl at Texas Stadium, but to be there that day was almost like being in one."

Smith had begun the day 93 yards short of the mark. He had picked up 11 on his second carry of the game, and the sellout crowd at Texas Stadium, which had come to see him do this more than they had come to see his Cowboys play Seattle, erupted. That crowd, which Smith would feed off all day, was every bit as ready for history as he was. And when the first quarter ended with Smith having rushed for 55 yards, they knew they would get it. "They," meaning the crowd, and Emmitt Smith. But when halftime came and Emmitt was still sitting on 55, everyone was still hopeful. They were no longer quite as sure.

The second quarter, from the point of view of Emmitt and the record chase, was a disaster. (The rest of us in the stadium had to keep reminding ourselves that there were also two teams out there trying to win a game.) The game was still scoreless as the quarter began with Emmitt losing a fumble, something that happened only slightly more often than the league's rushing record was broken. It was still scoreless when the Cowboys' third possession of the quarter started at their own 14 yard line, and on his next two carries, Emmitt lost a total of 7 yards. Suddenly Payton was gaining ground! In the second quarter Emmitt had four carries for a net gain of no yards plus a lost fumble.

Most of the third quarter was no better, but there was one difference: The Cowboys came out throwing the ball, and the crowd, which had come to see one thing and one thing only, booed. Poor Hutchinson couldn't win for losing. His first four plays of the second half were two incompletions, a 5-yard gain, and a sack. Now trailing 7–0, the Cowboys were finally able to eat up most of the last six minutes of the period with an 80-yard drive that included Emmitt's gains of 9, 5, 8, and 2 yards and ended with a touchdown pass to Galloway. The fourth quarter began with the game tied at 7–7, Seattle in possession of the ball, and Emmitt Smith 14 yards away from history.

Seattle scored about five minutes into the quarter, and by the time the Cowboys started their next possession down 14–7 at their own 27 yard line, everyone in the stadium, watching on television, or listening on the radio knew the number. The stadium scoreboard and public address announcer George Dunham had been tracking every needed yard since the third quarter, and so had Emmitt.

"There was a point," he remembers, "where I heard the announcer say whatever he said. 'Emmitt Smith needs so-and-so amount of yards. Emmitt Smith now needs 27 yards." (Not that that was the first update he heard, but it's one that stands out in his mind's ear.) "Then, I think the next number that jumped out might have been 13, something like that. But once that number started clicking down, it was like. . . ."

Apparently there are no words for what it was like, because Emmitt purses his lips and shudders at the very memory of it. "It was like I was trying to get it all in the first half, so we could get it over with and move on."

Campo had made it clear his top priority was winning the game. But the Cowboys head coach also knew the significance of the moment. And because he had been a member of the Cowboys coaching staff for Emmitt's entire career, he also knew there was no better way to serve both purposes than to feed it to number 22. There was no way Campo was having offensive coordinator Bruce Coslet call anything else.

On first and 10 at the 27, Smith carried off left tackle for 3. And then came the play that will adorn highlight films for all time. (The call on the Dallas Cowboys Radio Network: "Move over, Sweetness. Make a place for Emmitt.")

Funny, the way it looks in print. On the official NFL statistics and play by play sheet of the game, it reads: "2–7 DAL 30 (9:28)," which, for those of you who don't get the thrill of

Emmitt Smith exults after breaking the NFL all-time rushing record.

reading those sheets, means second down and 7 at the Dallas 30 with 9:28 to play in the quarter. "E. Smith left tackle to DAL 41 for 11 yards. Emmitt Smith passes Walter Payton as the National Football League's all-time career rushing leader. Payton's former record was 16,726 yards. Smith now has 16,728."

Just like that. But the words on the page don't begin to describe what the scene was like and what it meant to a legendary player and to his franchise.

As usual Emmitt knew exactly where he was. He bounced up, looking through the hole in the Texas Stadium roof as he held his arms outstretched, clutching the football in his left hand. As he leaped into the arms of his fullback, Thomas, flash-bulbs popped like firecrackers all over the stadium. The game stopped for a full five minutes as Emmitt found his family on the sideline, then former teammate Daryl Johnston, the glory-years fullback who had opened so many holes for so many thousands of those yards. Johnston was working the game as a FOX-TV analyst, and when Emmitt saw "Moose," he collapsed into Johnston's arms, and they embraced as only two warriors who have fought the same battle and survived can embrace.

And then, as is his wont, Emmitt Smith went back to work, because the Cowboys were still trailing 14–7 and there was still 9:05 to play.

The next carry went to the NFL's all time leading rusher. He lost a yard.

But two plays later, he skittered through the right side of the line for 14. And four plays after that, Emmitt Smith battered behind left tackle from the 1 yard line, and for the 150th time in his career, he rushed for a touchdown.

The Cowboys lost the game, by the way. Seattle took the ensuing kickoff and drove to a field goal with twenty-eight seconds remaining. It was the only thing that threatened to take the luster off the day. But because it was such an unusual day, it almost didn't matter. More than 20,000 people stayed in their seats after the game to watch the ceremony, to listen as Johnston, Summerall, Michael Irvin, and Hall of Famer Marcus Allen joined Jerry Jones in speaking in tribute to Smith, to watch as a banner proclaiming him the all-time rushing leader was unfurled from the rafters next to the five Super Bowl flags. The unfurling of that banner brought Emmitt Smith to tears.

How has all this changed Emmitt's life? "I find my greatest joy in holding the record when I hear people from across the country that I meet say to me, 'You deserve it.' Or, 'I'm glad you did it.' Or when I hear Chicago Bears fans say, 'I'm a big Bears fan, and Walter was my man, but if anyone in the National Football League deserved to break that record, it was you.' That makes me feel good. That makes me feel *very* good.

"I find joy when I find people telling me how they cried when I hugged Daryl Johnston the day I broke the record. That means a lot to me, because I feel like they felt *me*, how I feel about my teammates. That's really, really important to me.

"And it's funny, because it's now like I have fans in other lands." Chuckling at the wonderfully contradictory notion of it, he says, "I got a Philadelphia Eagle fan, boom! I got a Raider fan. [In February] I was in 'Niner country getting nothing but love up there in 'Niner country. It's nice to know that my work over the last thirteen years and what I have accomplished recently have been respected outside of the game."

Which leads us to what happens next in the professional life of Emmitt Smith. He has won three Super Bowl rings, four NFL rushing championships, a league MVP award, and a Super Bowl MVP. Now he is the preeminent ballcarrier in the

Emmitt Smith spoke to fans after the game in which he became the NFL's all-time leading rusher.

game's history, with more carries (4,052) for more yards (17,162) than anyone who has ever played. Even some of his former teammates wonder why he doesn't retire to enjoy his beautiful family and his ever growing love for golf. What continues to drive him?

"What drives me," he responds with no hesitation, so you know he's given this some thought, "is that I want to win. I want to go back to the Super Bowl because I want to be a champion all over again. And I just want to continue to play the game that I love as long as I can play it."

He also admits to a desire to reach 20,000 yards. Why? "Why not? I admit there are some things I can't do now. But I

Shy of a Grand

Emmitt Smith led the Cowboys in rushing in 2002 with 975 yards. The last time the Cowboys' leading rusher had fewer than 1,000 yards was Emmitt's rookie season, 1990. He finished that year with 937 yards.

can still make people miss me. I can still fall forward. Why 20,000 yards? Because it's there to be gotten. And I think I'm just the man to do it."

Unfortunately for Cowboys fans and purists, he won't be doing it in silver and blue. In February, citing salary cap constraints and the need to turn the page, the Cowboys released Emmitt, as so many NFL teams have done with trusted veterans in recent years. In late March Smith signed with the Arizona Cardinals. Everyone said all the right things. His parting press conference in Dallas was a classy hug-fest with Jerry Jones, and the Cardinals have talked about him as a man who can lend credibility to a franchise short on that commodity.

Emmitt wants to play, and the Cardinals will give him the chance. The odds are, though, that he will no more be thought of as a Cardinal than Joe Namath was a Ram or Johnny Unitas a Charger.

Emmitt Smith broke The Record as a Cowboy, and… sorry, Cardinals… a Cowboy he will always be.

When "the Thing" Wears a Star

"It requires a special individual to play it. He has to have a lot of things besides the physical skills to survive what now has become this 'Thing' that he faces every Sunday, and after the game, and on Mondays at the press conferences. It takes a special individual to do that."

—Dallas Cowboys head coach Bill Parcells at his introductory news conference, January 2, 2003

"It" is the quarterback position. The people who play it, forgiven a bias, will tell you it is the hardest position to play in sports.

Legend has it that two late Hall of Famers in different sports, contemporaries and cronies, used to spar about the most difficult feat in sports. Ted Williams, regarded by many as baseball's greatest hitter ever, used to chide golf icon Sam Snead. Williams reportedly insisted that hitting a baseball was the hardest thing an athlete could try to do. "Maybe," Snead is said to have retorted, "but after you hit it, you don't have to go chase it around."

Williams may have been right when it came to the difficulty of hitting a baseball. But it's a difficulty not limited to one position. The things an NFL quarterback must do just to survive, let alone excel, may well dwarf the demands put on

any other single position in any sport (we'll permit a debate from NHL goaltenders, but this isn't a hockey book).

Troy Aikman wore a star on his helmet for twelve seasons in a career that will land him in the Pro Football Hall of Fame. He was also an outstanding high school baseball player, good enough to have secured a pro offer from the New York Mets before deciding to play college football at the University of Oklahoma (and later, of course, UCLA). Aikman may not be objective, but he has a pretty good perspective when he says, "I think the position in and of itself carries tremendous pressure for those thirty-two guys who start each Sunday. For some there's a little bit more pressure than others, just based on their team, where they're at in their careers, and other factors."

The other factors are what this story is about. All quarterbacks are not created equal, and neither is the quarterback position on every team. We'll submit here that there are some teams for which playing the most demanding position in sport can devour a man who's not equal to the task.

You can make your own list of those teams. I've made mine. It's a list of teams who have such a rich legacy of success not just overall but at quarterback, especially, that any young man who steps under center is competing not just against the other team, but against the ghosts of the men who have succeeded in that uniform before him.

Obviously, Dallas is near the top of my list. They may have to share the top with San Francisco. What Jeff Garcia has accomplished as a 49er is impressive enough by itself. When you consider he's done it in the immediate shadow of Steve Young and Joe Montana, it shoots up the chart to remarkable, because those two predecessors are looking over Garcia's shoulder into every huddle, fair or not. That doesn't even

Troy Aikman holds most of the Cowboys' all-time passing records.

factor in what today serves as the ancient history accomplishments of Frankie Albert, Y. A. Tittle, and John Brodie.

Similarly, the Green Bay Packers serve as a difficult address for whichever quarterback someday follows multiple MVP Brett Favre, because the essence of Bart Starr still hovers over the Frozen Tundra as well.

Sometimes just one quarterback can cast such a long shadow as to make life tougher for whoever comes along later and is good enough to call up comparisons. In Denver, fair or not, you don't hear much about Craig Morton, who took the Broncos to the Super Bowl (something he couldn't quite do in Dallas), but it's John Elway the fans and media will not soon forget. In Miami Dan Marino was so great and so popular, the fact that he never won a championship won't matter to all the passers who try to make the Dolphins their own. Around the New York Jets, young Chad Pennington found out in 2002 that thirty-three years wasn't enough time for the franchise to outgrow the legend of Joe Willie Namath.

That's it. That's my list. San Francisco, Green Bay, Denver, Miami, the New York Jets. And Dallas. This story is about how tough it is when "the Thing" wears a star on its helmet.

Babe Laufenberg knows a little something about playing quarterback. So many colleges wanted him, he went to three (he claims Indiana but never lets you forget he was Elway's first roommate at Stanford). I'm allowed to kid Babe because he's my partner on the Cowboys radio broadcasts. But reality is he was good enough to play eight seasons in the NFL. He played on good teams and bad, behind and with some Hall of Famers: Joe Theismann, Aikman, Dan Fouts.

It was his San Diego and Dallas experiences that helped Laufenberg appreciate the differences between playing the position in a pressure cooker and just trying to play the position. "I went through it in San Diego," he recalls. "Fouts retired and I started the next year, in '88. Started the first six games before I broke my ribs. But I never had the sense that 'You're replacing this guy.' And hey, if they didn't like me, they'd go sailing. Here, if they don't like you, they'll bury you.

"Maybe part of that is that I wasn't there for five years, like Danny White was in Dallas when he replaced Roger Staubach. I don't even think when Troy came in he felt that pressure. He felt it more because the head coach [Jimmy Johnson] also brought in a guy who had helped him win a national [college] championship [Steve Walsh, at the University of Miami]. And the team was poor. But as soon as Troy started to become Troy Aikman, now it's 'who's better?'

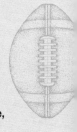

Expect the Best

The Cowboys have sent five different quarterbacks to the Pro Bowl through the years: Eddie LeBaron, Don Meredith, Roger Staubach, Danny White, and Troy Aikman.

"I don't think Troy ever thought about it then. I don't think there was a day in his first couple of years [when Laufenberg was his backup] that it ever occurred to him on the practice field, in a meeting room, walking through Valley Ranch, 'Okay, what would Roger have done?' Or, 'I have to live up to Roger.' Until someone mentioned Roger's name."

Which they started doing pretty quickly, and then Aikman got a taste of what it means to be not just an NFL quarterback, but the Quarterback of the Dallas Cowboys.

In retrospect he agrees that "there are not very many [teams] where there's been some sort of legacy at the position to where then as that quarterback you feel more pressure than what you would feel at other places. I think it's especially true for someone who is immediately succeeding that guy. Brian Griese in Denver, Danny [White] here in Dallas, [Jay] Fiedler following [Dan] Marino in Miami. Those are definite situations where people immediately compare you to that guy."

And those are tough situations. But Aikman is too modest to say publicly that he believed himself worthy of continuing the Staubach legend, and never mind that there were three starters in between them (White, Gary Hogeboom, and Steve Pelleur).

Another of Aikman's peers, though, understands as Laufenberg did that dropping in among the legends requires some serious mental toughness. Jason Garrett had already taken his Princeton education to the World League of American Football (the forerunner of the current NFL Europe) and the Canadian League, plus a stop on the New Orleans Saints' practice squad, before joining the Cowboys as a backup in 1992. He would stay in Dallas eight years and is now in his fourth season backing up Kerry Collins with the New York Giants.

Garrett got his first chance to play in Dallas in 1993, when Aikman was injured. "The overwhelming feeling that I had," he says, "I think every quarterback in this league feels a tremendous amount of pressure to perform, to be successful, to be a leader, to do what you need to do on Sundays. It's not an easy job. When you add to that the fact that this is a team that won the Super Bowl the year before, a team that has maybe the league's marquee player at the time playing that position, there was a tremendous amount of expectation to continue to be successful. Suddenly, he's taken out of the mix and you're in the mix. You're the variable. Now all that stuff I just mentioned [is magnified]. The Cowboys are *the Cowboys*. Every game you play is done [on television] by John Madden and Pat

One for the Ages

Jason Garrett was the Cowboys' third-string quarterback in 1994, but when both Troy Aikman and Rodney Peete were injured, Garrett started on Thanksgiving Day. He responded with a career day: more than 300 yards passing and two touchdowns in a 42–31 win over Green Bay.

Summerall. It was a national audience. It's a high profile position to begin with. Then, when you're on a team that's at the top of its game, it's playing shortstop for the Yankees, playing quarterback for the Cowboys. It's that position. There's less pressure when the team isn't good around you, when it's 'whatever happens, happens.' This team and this quarterback were great. You've got to keep this thing going.

"When you first go in, and this is my personal approach, you're just thinking, 'Prepare yourself. You're not Troy Aikman. You'll never be Troy Aikman. Play the way you play, execute, get the other players around you involved,' all those thoughts. But when you step back from it, it's [Don] Meredith, Staubach, Aikman. If you thought about that when you're playing, you wouldn't be able to play very well. It's a big plane to fly. There's nothing like it. It's an opportunity I will never forget in my lifetime."

Eddie LeBaron was the Cowboys' first quarterback in their expansion season, 1960. But with all apologies to Eddie, he didn't begin the mystique of the Cowboys Quarterback. That really started with Don Meredith. As tough as Staubach and Aikman were, Meredith was every bit their match in that department. What he didn't have was a powerhouse team around him for too many years. Meredith was a rookie and LeBaron's backup in 1960. He didn't claim the job as his own until 1963, and he retired in the spring of 1969. He was awfully good, but on a team still trying to climb the football mountain, he almost certainly never got the credit he deserved.

That's why the job Staubach left to Danny White in 1980 was a far different one from what Roger and Morton inherited in 1969. "It was the beginning of what Don had started to create," Staubach agrees. "I had a period of time where I was part of the Cowboys that Don Meredith created, and then I was very instrumental in the period beginning in 1975 when we got Randy White and that group, and then Tony Dorsett came in '77."

There are a lot of similarities between Aikman and Staubach. One of them is that it's difficult to keep them talking about themselves. Aikman always wants to talk about Michael Irvin and Jay Novacek and Emmitt Smith and his offensive line. Staubach will go on and on about the players around him, and that's part of Jason Garrett's point. In fact it's a point all the quarterbacks make, and maybe that's what makes a great quarterback: the better the players, the better the team. The better the team, the better the quarterback. But when "the Thing" has a star on its helmet, you better, in the words of Tiger Woods, bring your "A" game. And it was Staubach who got that started.

"It's a history thing," he says. "Over the decades we were on TV a lot, and people knew us. But it was Don Meredith and Bob Hayes who created the wide-open, exciting Cowboys era. Then in the '80s we kind of hung in there, and then Troy and those guys resurrected the Cowboys in the '90s, so it's a three-decade thing. Our decade kind of began that interest in the Cowboys because of all the TV exposure and the star on the helmet and

Roger Staubach became known as "Captain Comeback." An opponent once called him "Captain America."

the TV show *Dallas*. And we were a heck of a football team. We were exciting, and we were a controversial team. And Tom [Landry] was the symbol. People were intrigued with him."

And what does Staubach think he was the symbol of? "I think I was a by-product of that success because I was the quarterback. I fought like crazy on the field, and off the field I don't have any skeletons. I'm not a hypocrite, I don't try to be something I'm not, and I think people associate me with the positive things Coach Landry [embodied]. The quarterback gets the status. And there was the 'America's team' thing. I remember [playing Philadelphia] when [Eagles linebacker] Bill Bergey knocked the hell out of me, knocked the wind out of me, and when he helped me off the ground, he said, 'Take that, Captain America.' "

In light of what Staubach has come to mean to the Cowboys and their fans, it's almost unbelievable that he and Craig Morton were involved in one of the most bizarre chapters in the team's quarterback history. It's also another bit of evidence that as great as he was, Landry frequently had a tough time getting a handle on managing the key position on the field.

Craig Morton had been an All-American at California and was the team's first draft choice, the sixth overall pick, in 1965. Staubach finished his Navy obligations and joined the team in 1969, just when Meredith had stunned the club by retiring. Morton was the starter in 1969 and 1970, when the Cowboys made their first Super Bowl appearance (a 16–13 loss to Baltimore in Super Bowl V).

Landry couldn't make up his mind between the two for the 1971 season, though, which is why, as Staubach recalls, "We were alternating games. Tom announced we were going to have two starting quarterbacks. I was supposed to start the opener, but I hurt my leg in the last exhibition game against the Chiefs, so I had to sit out, and Craig started against Buffalo. Craig started and had a great game, and the next week I started against the Eagles, and that friggin' chicken defensive end [Mel Tom] hit me from behind in the head, knocked me out . . . a dirty shot . . . and I'm out two weeks. Craig started against the Saints, and we lost, but I came in [in] the fourth quarter and we scored twice. Then I started the first game at Texas Stadium, against New England, and we had a big win.

"So now we have this controversy. It's all anybody's talking about and everyone's taking sides. So now we sit in our team meeting, and Tom gets up and says, 'Here's what we're going to do this week [against Chicago]: Roger and Craig are going to alternate plays. I looked over at Craig [he laughs again at the memory] and said, 'Is this guy crazy? Did he have a concussion? What the hell is Tom doing? Did he have a lobotomy?' That deal didn't work out [the Cowboys lost on Halloween 23–19], and we actually quit alternating plays in the fourth quarter and Craig stayed in. I thought, 'I'm toast again.' But the next week changed my life. I thought he was going to go with Craig again, but he announced I would be the starting quarterback the rest of the year."

That turned out to be one of Landry's better moves. The Cowboys, under Staubach, won their final seven games, beat Minnesota and San Francisco in the playoffs, and won their first Super Bowl championship, 24–3 against Miami, on January 16, 1972.

It was the birth of "the Thing" in Dallas.

There may be no better example of the existence of "the Thing" than the thirteen-year Cowboys career of Danny White. You don't want to be the one who follows the legend; you want to be the one who follows the one who followed the legend. But White, who joined the Cowboys in 1976 from

Danny White (11) may have been the Cowboys' most underappreciated quarterback.

Memphis of the abortive World League, was a more than ready heir apparent when Staubach was forced into retirement by a mounting concussion count after the 1979 season. In his first three years as the starter, Danny White quarterbacked the Cowboys to the NFC Championship Game. I've never heard of another quarterback who did that.

Yet in the public perception, the Cowboys' quarterbacking royalty goes from Staubach to Aikman. White is remembered as the one who didn't go to the Super Bowl, the one Landry benched for Gary Hogeboom after a *Dallas Morning News* poll of players showed the cannon-armed Hogey was the players' choice. More than anything, that vote probably had to do with White's role in the players' strike of 1982. He had circumvented the team's union membership to negotiate directly with general manager Tex Schramm, arguably the most powerful man in the NFL at the time. White was dissatisfied with the lack of movement in labor talks, but many players saw his action as self-serving. It damaged White's relationship with some of his teammates beyond repair.

"I'm a Danny White fan," says Staubach, "but Danny didn't have control of the team the way he should, and that showed. When they did that poll, if that had happened on my watch, I'd have been in a fight with those guys in the locker room. I know who those guys were. They were copping out, trying to push the blame off on someone else. Danny didn't have a total connection with all of them. But he was a good guy and a hell of a football player. He just needed to take control of those guys. I wouldn't put up with stuff like that. I would've been ballistic on something like that."

Fans didn't know too much about those details, though, nor did they care. White was just the guy who followed Staubach and didn't go to the Super Bowl. That's the key point about White, who today is the head coach of the Arizona Rattlers of the Arena Football League.

"I don't know if it was so much following Roger or following the Super Bowls," he says. "That's what it's really all about. I think what it came down to was that the *team* had great success. It wouldn't have mattered much who followed whom, I don't think, except for the team results. Roger has said many times, a quarterback is more dependent than any other position in sports on the people around him. No one else—not a pitcher, not a point guard, I don't care who it is—has to rely so much on the people around him.

"The thing that made Roger Staubach great was not his arm, not his ability to read defenses, not his scrambling. The thing that set him apart was his ability to get the most out of the guys around him. He was absolutely unyielding on what he expected of the people around him. I wasn't as vocal as Roger. If I have a regret, it's that I didn't stand up on occasion and say, 'This is how it's going to be, and this is what we're going to do. Take it or leave it. I am what I am and this is how it's going to be.' Roger would have done that. That was the biggest difference in the two of us."

Still, benching White was a move Staubach calls Landry's "biggest mistake ever. Tom Landry is the best, but he fell for it."

So Troy Aikman became the guy who followed the guy. With his skill, demeanor, leadership, and relentless competitive drive, it wouldn't have mattered who he followed. For the record Aikman agrees that Danny White "had a fabulous career. He doesn't get recognized for what he accomplished. But ultimately, it was because he didn't win a Super Bowl because he immediately followed Roger Staubach. There have been other players who had great careers and didn't win Super Bowls, and they're not slighted. Maybe it was that Roger was so [much] larger than life."

Staubach was larger than life to Aikman, too, but Aikman had all he could do to survive his first couple of seasons on a team that had been bad enough to earn the right to draft him. "It didn't become a big deal to me until we began to win," he says. "Then people start talking about you in the same class, and then they start talking about what a rich tradition there is at the position with this franchise. That made me feel good.

"Roger to me is almost like a mythical figure. To me he's a

standard that can never be met. Even if it is met and even if it's surpassed, really, in the eyes of the historians, including myself, it's like . . . to me, he's like Joe DiMaggio. Yeah, they can make comparisons, but it's not really fair. Roger always told me, 'Hey, don't worry about any of that. Once you retire, they only remember the good things.' And I've already realized that. But it's a comparison that I never really felt comfortable with."

He may as well start getting comfortable with it. Aikman early on met Bill Parcells' requirements for playing quarterback in the big time: "You

It Ain't Me

Every moment of Troy Aikman's Hall of Fame career wasn't for the highlight reel. In one game in his rookie season, he broke the huddle and lined up under right guard Crawford Ker, who looked back over his shoulder and croaked, "It ain't me, Daddy!"

don't find out if a guy can play quarterback in the NFL until he got beat 35–7, he threw four interceptions, he's clearly the reason you lost. He got his nose broken, the fans are booing, the press is on his ass, the coaches are looking at him sideways, and on Wednesday, he's got to get his team back in the huddle."

It's never been harder to play quarterback in the NFL than it is today. As Laufenberg says, "You have zone blitzes, things we never had to worry about. And teams reach for guys. They take a guy in the top five, top ten who should've gone in the second round, but now he's got to play right away. What do they think is gonna happen to the guy? It's like eating your young."

That's "the Thing," and thanks to Staubach and Aikman, especially, it's worse when "the Thing" wears a star.

The Best Loss

There's supposed to be no such thing.

A "good loss" in professional football is thought to be an oxymoron. Sometimes, admittedly, they seem to exist. Although no one ever wants to lose a game, occasionally a team will get on an early roll, maybe get a little full of itself, relax a bit subconsciously, and get knocked off its perch while there's still time in the season to recover. This is thought to be a good loss. Longtime followers of the early Cowboys used to swear that Tom Landry liked to have his team knocked on its back around midseason so he could regain its total attention in practice and meetings for the stretch run.

But you'll never get a player or a coach to admit that. If a cocky team is made hungrier and more humble by a defeat, or if a team searching for its personality overachieves against a supposedly better opponent and finds in that result the motivation to play well, you'll still never hear a player or coach in the NFL agree that it was a good loss. What you usually hear is a grumbled, "You don't learn anything from losing."

But it's not true. There are losses, and then there are losses. Sometimes you find the good losses in the strangest places.

For the dynasty Cowboys of the 1990s, there was such a game. The 38–28 defeat at the hands of the 49ers in the 1994 NFC Championship Game in San Francisco was their best loss.

Ask Troy Aikman, the Cowboys' future Hall of Fame quarterback, to select a defining moment for his career, a game that sums up what he was all about, and he picks that game. "I hope that game defined what I was," Aikman recalls. "I think a lot of people up to that time had only seen or remembered me and the team in favorable situations and winning games. It wasn't always like that. They didn't see the 1–15 season [in 1989] and what it took to get to the championships. Now we're on the national stage, and we had our backs to the wall for the first time in most people's minds, and we kept battling. I was proud of the way I played the game and continued to compete, and I was proud of the way our team competed."

Aikman's not the only one. Joe Avezzano was the Cowboys' special teams coach from 1990 to 2002, and he became one of Aikman's closest friends. Aikman still talks about the tough times of his second year, Avezzano's first with the team. Many were the Sunday nights after a tough loss (that's what losses are supposed to be, you know) that Aikman would go to Avezzano's house, where Joe's wife, Diane, would whip up some of her famous homemade pasta, and Aikman would unburden himself. Today, more than two years after Aikman's retirement, Avezzano still marvels at what he saw that January day in 1995.

"He was always a tough son of a gun," Avezzano says. "But what we saw that day was like nothing I've ever seen. The 49ers were beating the crap out of him all day, and he kept getting up and coming back. I've told him many times, I've never been prouder of him in any other game.

"On the grass field, in the mud, with sod sticking out of his helmet, he just kept throwing. I remember one time he was coming to the sideline during a timeout. The sunlight and the shadows hit him just right, and I remember thinking, all we needed was the voice of John Facenda [the original legendary voice of NFL Films] coming down from the sky to explain to

Troy Aikman, muddy but unbowed, fires away against San Francisco in the 1994 NFC Championship Game.

us how this battered and beaten quarterback had brought his team back from the brink of defeat. It was unparalleled. He was gallant in his efforts."

But this is not just a story about Troy Aikman and his toughness. It's a story about a championship team that proved its mettle, even in a game it didn't win with a Super Bowl appearance at stake. Aikman and Avezzano are not the only ones with memories of that game that still get the blood flowing.

Few players had more memorable moments in Cowboys' blue and silver than Emmitt Smith, who became the NFL's all-time rushing leader in October 2002, breaking Walter Payton's record. Smith gained a national reputation for toughness with a season-ending game against the Giants in 1993 in which he carried the load for two and a half quarters with a separated shoulder. He was the Super Bowl MVP a month later in Atlanta against Buffalo. But ask Emmitt Smith to list his favorite games in his Dallas career, and he begins with, "Probably the '94 championship game that we lost." And why is that?

"Because even in defeat, and as hard as it was to accept that defeat, I felt something. I don't want to say the previous two years the games came easy, but we were so good, it appeared to be easy. And that third year we weren't so bad, but we had adversity hit us, to a degree where we almost lost a player. [Pro Bowl tackle Erik Williams was lost for the season in an automobile wreck.] Not only that, but we had lost the mystique of the head coach [Jimmy Johnson had left the team in March of that year, replaced by the beleaguered Barry Switzer]. That was shouldered by the leaders on the ball club. Those leaders, those lions, raised up their heads and said

You Again?

Since the NFL–AFL merger in 1970, the Cowboys have appeared in fourteen NFC Championship Games. Six of those have been against San Francisco. Dallas's record in those games is 4–2. In championship game competition Dallas is also 1–1 versus Minnesota, 1–1 versus the Los Angeles Rams, 0–2 versus Washington, 0–1 versus Philadelphia, and 1–0 versus Green Bay.

'We're not going to let this happen to us. So we're going to fight.' And we fought as hard as we could. That [game] might have been one of the proudest moments of my thirteen-year career, just to see that actually happen. That to me defined the true team concept."

At this point we need a scene-setter, and Smith has gotten us started. In 1994 the Cowboys were two-time defending Super Bowl champions, and in both of those years, 1992 and 1993, they had beaten San Francisco in the NFC Championship Game, once in San Francisco, once in Texas Stadium. In 1994 they had finished 12–4, but they had lost two of the last three games, and one of their other losses had come in San Francisco on November 13. That's why the championship game was back at Candlestick Park.

The Cowboys regained their swagger with a 35–9 divisional playoff win over Green Bay at home, so they went back to San Francisco not much caring about the venue. But they were beaten up. Smith played with a tight hamstring. Williams had been replaced at right tackle by rookie Larry Allen, who had an ankle injury so bad he probably shouldn't have played. But the remaining three linemen on the bench (Dale Hellestrae, Frank Cornish, and Ron Stone) were more centers and guards. So Allen, who has gone on to seven Pro Bowls since, limped out there.

Safety Darren Woodson, now a five-time Pro Bowl player, was in his second year as a starter in 1994. He was one of the walking wounded that day. "In the training room before that game," Woodson recalls, "I don't think I've seen so many needles in my life. I had a bad back. Larry Allen had the high ankle sprain. I remember on Thursday of that week being in the training room and every table was full. Guys could not practice. Troy had hit his hand on someone's helmet. On game day I'm there getting shot up, Larry's getting shot up, and I remember me thinking the whole time that we're gonna go out and kill 'em."

So the injuries were of no great concern. They were the two-time defending Super Bowl champions, after all. Wide receiver Michael Irvin, who had just been named to his fourth Pro Bowl, had been waiting for this game all year.

"Going into the season," Irvin remembers, "we were hearing all about the split up between [owner] Jerry [Jones] and Jimmy, and Jimmy is the reason we won the Super Bowls. It's all about Jimmy. Now you know I love Jimmy to death, and he was a big reason. But I thought to myself, 'We have to show the world we can win a Super Bowl without Jimmy.' The whole season that's all I thought about. Going into that game, the 49ers had added Deion [Sanders, the Pro Bowl corner-back]. So now I get the opportunity to play on the major stage against Deion Sanders, one of the best cornerbacks in the game. So I couldn't wait to play this game. Could not wait to play this game. It's the one game you live through every season for. I remember at one of the press conferences, they asked me what did I think would happen. I told them, 'When we were getting ready to go to the airport, I kissed my wife and said, "Baby, we're going to win a game." I didn't kiss my wife and say we're going all the way to San Francisco to lose. We came to win a game.' We were confident we were going to win. Maybe too confident."

At this point it seems only fair to point out that the 49ers were also pretty good. Just ask the San Diego Chargers, who fell to them in the ensuing Super Bowl 49–26. These were the 49ers of Steve Young, Jerry Rice, Brent Jones, Dana Stubble-field, Merton Hanks, former Cowboy Ken Norton Junior, and, oh, yes, Deion Sanders.

As Babe Laufenberg, my radio broadcast partner and a former quarterback, says, "That may be the last great game that we see like that, because it may be the last time there are two extremely talented teams, both sides of the ball, with Hall of Fame athletes. Not just great athletes or good players or Pro Bowl players, [but] Hall of Fame players stacked up deep for both teams. The salary cap has kind of taken that out of the equation now. Those are two teams that would beat any team playing football today, or, I venture to say, over the last five years. Those two teams would have beaten them all by twenty points. And they were players that had played together for a number of years. Steve Young, Jerry Rice, Troy Aikman, Michael Irvin, Emmitt Smith, all Hall of Fame players in the prime of their careers."

Famous

The Cowboys' first-ever NFC Championship Game appearance was against San Francisco in January 1971. Seven players from that game are now in the Hall of Fame: from Dallas, Herb Adderley, Mike Ditka, Bob Lilly, Mel Renfro, and Roger Staubach (plus GM Tex Schramm and coach Tom Landry). From SF: Jimmy Johnson and Dave Wilcox.

It was the kind of day you get playing football in mid-January in San Francisco: dank, partly cloudy 52 degrees at game time, with the grass-and-kitty-litter-like surface at "the 'Stick" coming up in clumps under the feet of those great players. And the day began like no day in recent memory for the Dallas Cowboys.

The 49ers kicked off, and on the third play of the game, cornerback Eric Davis stepped in front of a pass intended for Dallas's slot receiver Kevin Williams and returned it 44 yards for a touchdown. Says Aikman: "They disguised their defense real well. We were in three wides with the slot on the right. They played a trap coverage where Eric Davis ran out with the outside receiver and then cut back in. That was just good defense on their part."

After the touchdown and the next kickoff, Emmitt Smith lost 3 yards when he slipped in the mud on a first down run and 4 more on an aborted screen pass. On third and 17, Aikman hit Irvin for 16 yards, but Irvin uncharacteristically fumbled when he was hit by Davis. Irvin takes all the blame.

"Oh, man," Irvin moans, wearing an expression of pain eight years after the fact. "Yeah, I remember running the route, saying to myself, 'Get enough for the first down.' If I catch the ball right at the marker, I can get another yard. Actually, I was probably a yard short, because I had to reach back to catch the ball. . . . I cut in a little quick, and the ball was behind me when I caught it. If I had gone another yard, it would have hit me in the chest, and I could have cradled it and fell. . . . As I reached behind me and caught it, the ball was still on my back hip where Eric was, and he swatted it down and knocked it out.

"As I hit the ground, I thought to myself, 'Oh please, call this down.' I knew it was a fumble. I was shocked. It was my favorite route, a '4' route, a deep in. My favorite route by far. Any time there's a third and over 15, I'm always yelling, 'Let's throw that four.' "

The 49ers recovered at the Dallas 39. Young completed a fourth down and 2 pass to tight end Ted Popson, and on the next play running back Ricky Watters took a swing pass 24 yards down the sideline for another touchdown.

At this point none of the Cowboys was overly worried yet. "I'm still thinking, 'It's cool, so we spot them 14,' " says Irvin.

But Kevin Williams fumbled the next kickoff. The 49ers went 35 yards in seven plays. Fullback William Floyd plugged

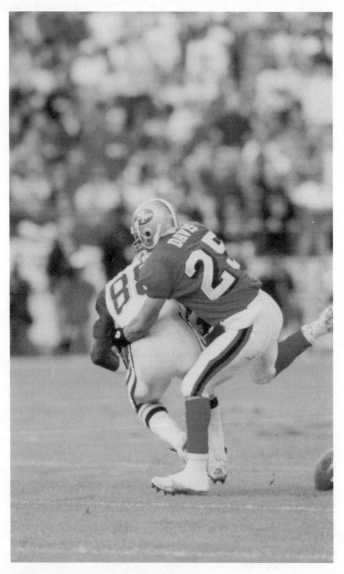

Michael Irvin (88) is stripped of the ball (lower right) by the Niners'
Eric Davis.

in the last yard, and the 49ers led the NFC Championship Game 21–0. The game was seven minutes and twenty-seven seconds old.

Now, there were some concerns.

Recalls Woodson: "The feeling on the sideline was like a dream, almost, a bad dream. I was so young, I was still thinking, 'Well, '8' [Aikman] can get us there.' But at 21–0 I didn't know what to think."

Irvin did. "Now, I'm worried. I'm thinking, okay the first [turnover] I can understand, the second one . . . , but now when that happened on the kickoff, I thought, 'Something's funny here. Like it's not meant to be. This is not cool at all.' "

Aikman: "Those of us who had been around in '89 and '90 had been in games where suddenly you're down a bunch, and having been in those kinds of games, whatever tension you had going in was now gone. Then it's like sandlot ball. You've just got to start making plays. We started throwing some balls in some situations that in a close game you're not going to risk throwing."

But fullback Daryl Johnston had another concern. "There's something psychological about 21–0," Johnston says. "It's so hard to score touchdowns in the NFL. The red zone is such a tough area to move the football in. I think one of the reasons we were good is that we could run the ball in the red zone. But we were not a big play team. We took the approach that if you're going to try and defend our deep ball, with Michael and Alvin [Harper] and Jay [Novacek], we'll just run the ball with Emmitt. When you find yourself down twenty-one, you're talking, for us, three drives. We weren't the St. Louis Rams. We had potential to have big plays, and we had a number of them, but we were known as a team that could move the ball in eight-to-twelve-play drives. The one thing that saved us was that [it happened so fast], we still have time to keep our game plan. We don't have to get out of our game right now.

"But the biggest thing to me was that we could never get inside of ten points. If we could have ever gotten it to seven, I think for them, it's a double whammy. Now, we've got confidence because we're one drive, one play. And for them, 'Gosh,

Fullback Daryl Johnston knows it's going to be a long day in the 1994 NFC Championship Game at San Francisco.

we just let a three-touchdown lead go.' I think the combined thing switches to our favor. But we could never get inside ten."

But oh, how they tried. Despite being down 21–0, Aikman led the Cowboys on an eight-play, 62-yard drive to an Irvin touchdown reception. The Cowboys' Chris Boniol missed a second-quarter field goal; Doug Brien kicked one for San Francisco to make the lead 24–7. Dallas cut it to ten with a Smith touchdown. The 49ers pushed it back to seventeen with a Young-to-Rice score just before halftime, a touchdown that nearly broke the Dallas spirit. But only nearly.

Dave Campo, later a Cowboys head coach, was the secondary coach in 1994. Woodson remembers him telling the defensive backs at halftime, "It's not about what the score is. It's about who's gonna fight. We've been in this situation before as a secondary. Now, are we going to be scrappy and fight?"

The teams traded third-quarter touchdowns, but Dallas made a gallant fourth quarter stand, and it is that fourth quarter that makes the game stand out in so many memories. An 89-yard Cowboys drive ended with Aikman's second touchdown pass to Irvin, and the Dallas defense, making its best stand of the day, forced the 'Niners three and out. Woodson and the defense hoped that might be the turning point.

"Our offense had fought so hard that whole game," he says, "and I remember the momentum changing throughout the game."

Dallas still had that ten-point deficit with 7:18 to play and the ball at its own 26. Five plays and a 49ers penalty later, it was second and 10 at the SF 43. What followed may not have been the most important play of the game, but it remains the most controversial.

Irvin was the target of an Aikman pass deep down the left sideline. He was also the target of contact from Sanders. Eight years later, everyone connected with the Cowboys knows to his core Sanders interfered, but no penalty was called.

Well, that's not quite right. Switzer, incensed at the absence of a flag, ran onto the field, confronted the officials, and drew an unsportsmanlike penalty. Instead of third and 10 at the 43, it was third and 25 back at the Dallas 42.

Any Cowboy you can find will talk your ear off about that play and how it turned the game. But let's let Irvin do the honors.

"We're running a '787 pump.' I run a deep out, expecting Deion to jump the out, which he did. I turn upfield and go. The ball hung up just a little bit, which is dangerous with Deion because of his great recovery speed. I remember him jumping, and *bam*, I was in back of him. He turns, he's running, I'm waiting on the ball, he reaches out to catch up with me. Grabs my arm because he's thinking I'm reaching out to catch the ball now. But he's early. Even in the picture you can see he's got my arm and I'm reaching out trying to catch the ball with my other hand. But they never made the call."

To a man the Cowboys believe had they gotten that call, they would have scored, and that if they had scored, they'd have won. We didn't ask any 49ers their opinion, but I expect they'd disagree.

It doesn't matter. What matters is what the game meant to the people in it. For Aikman: "This was a lot of guys' first opportunity since 1–15 to really have our backs to the wall and to say, 'Okay, now let's see how guys react.' I think it exemplifies why we were so successful in '92 and '93 and '95. The core of the team was those kinds of guys." It's a theme echoed by Irvin, Johnston, Smith, Woodson, all of them. We never quit, even down 21–0 in the first quarter. We kept fighting.

It took Troy Aikman a couple of years to appreciate that game. "We felt terrible about the chance we'd missed. But so many people in the years since have commented that they finally saw us battle adversity, and they appreciated how hard we fought back in that game."

It didn't take Johnston that long. "I was in Del Frisco's [a popular Dallas steakhouse] about a week later having dinner," he offers. "I was actually there with a friend and his mom and dad who were diehard 'Niner fans. When we got up to leave, people got up to give me a standing ovation. I think not only the team, but the town realized what had happened that day, that here was a group of guys who were not going to quit, and if you don't put them away, they'll get you."

For Babe Laufenberg, the Best Loss was "the essence of athletic competition. We're gonna break you physically and we're gonna break you mentally. But they [the 'Niners] just couldn't break 'em. It was like a boxer. After all I've thrown at him, this guy still wants to fight? Are you kidding me? I know San Francisco was saying, what do we have to do to make these guys quit? And it wasn't happening."

And it never did. Even more than winning, it's what football is all about.

Once More,
with Tuna

If it were really just about business for Jerry Jones, he'd have taken that Chargers deal back in 1965.

It's a story he's told before, and he still gets some strange enjoyment from the retelling. Jones is like this, by the way: Many of his illustrations involve recounting of his "might-have-beens."

But sitting in his office at the team headquarters at Valley Ranch, the Cowboys owner and general manager remembers, with some prodding, that his purchase of the Dallas Cowboys in 1989 was not his first inquiry into ownership in the NFL.

When he was coming out of the University of Arkansas almost forty years ago, Jones was trying to find his business niche. "I didn't have any money," he says, "but I had some people who were interested enough in the AFL situation that they were going to loan me the money. My dad didn't like where I was getting the money, but we shouldn't get into that." (Rumor has it it was the Teamsters Union. Jones only smiles.)

"These people were going to loan me some money to build some pizza parlors. Daddy said, 'Does it work?' I said, 'No, they don't make any money.' He said, 'You're gonna spend the next ten or fifteen years of your life working on something that doesn't make any money?' So I didn't. But the Chargers deal, $50,000 tied it up for 120 days, with an option at $5.8

million. The NFL and AFL wound up merging in sixty days, and the Chargers sold for $12 million."

So that $50,000 loan Jerry Jones, at his dad's urging, didn't take, turned into a $12 million profit. "For the rest of his life," Jones says laughing, "I reminded him of that advice. But it just shows that he didn't understand the dynamics—nor did I—of a sports franchise."

He Played, Too

Jerry Jones was a high school running back at North Little Rock (Arkansas) High, and was a guard and cocaptain of the University of Arkansas' unbeaten national championship team in 1964.

Obviously, three Super Bowl titles and two major rebuilding projects later, Jerry Jones understands those dynamics now. But this story is about what he did understand fourteen years ago when he embarked on the first rebuilding, and what he understands and believes more fiercely than ever as he launches into the next stage of franchise history.

What Jones has done and is doing is as fascinating as most other aspects of one of America's most studied sports icons. Because they are the Dallas Cowboys, nothing this team does seems mundane. Without question none of it escapes scrutiny and, frequently, controversy. When they win, they do it big, in ways that make you notice. When they lose, they don't mess around there either.

When Jones bought the Cowboys in February 1989, Dallas, Green Bay, Miami, and the Raiders had each won two Super Bowl titles. San Francisco had just won its third, and Pittsburgh had four. Today, of course, the 49ers and Cowboys have the most hardware. They're in a race to see who can become the first team to win six Lombardi Trophies.

But what Jones got when he wrote that first big check was not what he bought. And he knew it. The Dallas Cowboys in 1988 had finished 3–13, and looked bad doing it.

They'd had a losing record three seasons in a row and hadn't won a playoff game in six seasons, since falling to Washington in the NFC Championship Game in January 1983. That made it six seasons and light years away from NFL glory. The off-the-field picture wasn't much better. The team was hemorrhaging money.

That's what Jerry Jones got, and he knew all of it going in. But he also knew exactly what he was buying. He was buying, he confirms, "the image, the aura, the interest that the franchise represented. Coach [Tom] Landry, Tex [Schramm], the personalities, all of that is what moved me to purchase the team. It really wasn't there for me at that time for another team. I was inspired by the thing that Tex and Tom and Staubach represented, and what that was about. It was so real. I did believe in the power of pride and the power of motivation.

"I had experienced that in my life in sports at the college level [as a player on the University of Arkansas' national championship team]. I had seen young men get motivated above their abilities. I had been a part of teams that did that, so that was very meaningful to me.

"And I had seen in the business world the power of tradition and brand. The business world constantly draws on the sports world for its analogies. I couldn't quite put a numerical value on it, but I thought it was worth half of what I paid [estimated to be around $160 million], and it maybe would go at times to three-quarters of what I was buying was just the perception of what it might mean for a player to play for the Dallas Cowboys. I never considered as a negative the fact that the Cowboys were down. I never considered it. It was like they weren't even down. I was aware that they hadn't won the last two or three years, but it never was a consideration. It never occurred to me that we wouldn't win the football games with what we had to work with with the Dallas Cowboys."

There are some longtime fans who still wince when they hear Jones say these things. These are, one suspects, people who mostly have not forgiven Jones for replacing Landry with Jimmy Johnson, and there is nothing he can ever do to convince those people.

There are two ironies here. One is that Jones has been so excoriated for replacing Landry and is presumed to have had no regard for the coach's accomplishments. People who believe that may not know of Schramm's ambivalence about Landry's remaining on the job in what turned out to be his final few seasons. The team's second owner, Bum Bright, from whom Jones bought the team, was constantly after Schramm to change coaches. "He once offered me all of Landry's money if I'd fire him," Tex once said. They may also not know of Jones's high regard for Landry all along, of how long Landry rebuffed Jones's attempts to install him in the Texas Stadium Ring of Honor before he finally relented and accepted enshrinement in 1993.

The second irony is that the diehard Jonesphobes are almost always people who have never had the opportunity to spend any time with Jerry Jones. If you get that chance, it's impossible not to be convinced of his passion for winning and of his passion for the Dallas Cowboys.

Jones remembers a time in that 1989 season, which was an artistic disaster as the tearing down and rebuilding commenced, when the aura of what the Cowboys were was driven home to him again. It was done by the man he'd brought with him to help the return to NFL greatness, Jimmy Johnson.

Jerry Jones inducts Tom Landry (right) into the Ring of Honor in 1993.

Jones leans forward in his chair, tangibly warming to the subject. "One time I was visiting with Jimmy—this wasn't in front of people, this was just us talking—and we were kind of giving each other a little bit of a pep talk, although not deliberately. Jimmy said, 'Jerry, you know why we're gonna win? Not because of who we've got or don't have, not because of who we've got at quarterback or what have you. We're gonna win because we're the Dallas Cowboys.'"

If you've never been exposed to the Cowboys' culture, if you've never seen what an impact just the name has on people in and outside of Dallas–Fort Worth, you could be excused for taking that sentiment as sheer arrogance. But if you have had that exposure, you understand the motivation. As one who has been around the franchise for more than twenty-five years, I've long believed that Jerry Jones and Tex Schramm had more in common than either of them may have wished to admit. This belief that the Cowboys will prevail because they're the Cowboys is a shining example.

Schramm set out when he joined the Cowboys to create a mystique. He wanted to pattern it after the success enjoyed by the New York Yankees, and he did. It's ear catching to hear Jones talk in the same terms. "It never occurred to me," Jones says, "what was ahead over the next twelve or fifteen years relative to the financial aspects of the league or of the Cowboys. I knew I wanted to stop the bleeding and stop the losing money, although some of the opportunity didn't seem to be there at the time. But what I was looking at was that this reputation, this . . . in my frame of reference . . . this Notre Dame, would allow us to win football games, and allow us in some way, by hook or crook, to put teams together that would be at the top."

And did it?

"Yes, it did. There's no question it did. It inspired our coaching staff, inspired me. I mean, you immediately walked in, and unlike an expansion franchise or unlike other franchises in sports, you immediately walked in and sat down in your chair and said, 'Man, I'm a part of the Dallas Cowboys. I'm a part of the Yankees, a part of Notre Dame.' That caused you to just reach for it. In the early months and really first two or three years, there were significant obstacles that normally would have made you lay awake or just knock your feet out from under you. And it was just like little bitty raindrops rolling off your back. It created a confidence.

"When we had our first opportunity in free agency, under the old Plan B, with the team and the stadium still losing money, we spent more than anybody in the NFL in Plan B. That's where we got [tight end Jay] Novacek, and that's where we got [safety James] Washington, and that's where we got some of these players that really contributed. I remember sitting back there in the scouting office, and we had all our Plan B players listed on a board, and we had already spent X number of dollars. Jimmy and I were standing there talking about another tackle, and we were talking about another $100,000 or $150,000 then. I looked at the board and said, 'This guy hasn't signed yet?' Jimmy said, 'Nope.' I said, 'Well, let's get him.' Jimmy was actually trying to be conservative with my money. I was doing that with my right hand, while my left hand was trying to stop the bleeding and put a tourniquet on out here. That's what the Cowboys' tradition did to me."

To completely ascribe the Cowboys' success in any era to mystique would, of course, be ludicrous. Schramm might have been the NFL's all-time marketing genius, and he wouldn't

Not Him, the Other Guy

When Jerry Jones brought in a new coaching staff to Dallas in 1989, he got a call from old friend Lou Holtz, the former head coach at Notre Dame and Arkansas. Holtz congratulated Jones on hiring "the best young coach in America." He wasn't talking about Jimmy Johnson, though. Holtz was talking about new defensive coordinator Dave Wannstedt, who went on to be coach of the Chicago Bears and the Miami Dolphins.

have sold a suite at the stadium or a sponsorship or a T-shirt if he hadn't hired Landry and Staubach and Bob Lilly and Tony Dorsett and Randy White and so many others. Similarly, Jones might have been the swiftest business mind ever to come down the pike, but he'd have had nothing to market had he not brought in the likes of Johnson and Troy Aikman and Emmitt Smith and Michael Irvin. But Jones's point is that those players and coaches—and, although he doesn't say it, Schramm and Jones as well—are the mystique that breeds mystique. Once the early Cowboys got over the hump in the mid-1960s, the legend grew and became a beast of its own. And without question what Schramm, Landry, Gil Brandt, and their players started, the Cowboys of the Jones era have grown. If Jones bought, as he says, "Staubach, Landry, those names," what he now has is Staubach, Landry, Aikman, Smith, Irvin, Johnson, *those* names. So keeping in mind that he is presiding over a work in progress, has he in any measure done what he set out to accomplish?

The short answer, of course, is yes, and Jones (as Schramm before him) only laments what he got close to doing that would have been even better. He reviews recent history and says, "I thought three years ago when we brought in [receiver Joey] Galloway and [tight end Jackie] Harris, that we still had the opportunity, because of Troy Aikman, and in the lay of the land in free agency, to push this thing up to another Super Bowl season. There was a lot of the Cowboy thing going for us in my mind, pushing me along, but with that kind of experience and skills, I thought we had a chance.

"We had tried to see if Chan [Gailey]'s different offense would freshen things up around here, maybe take advantage of some things Troy could do with his experience that he might not have been doing with Ernie Zampese at the time. I thought

Former coach Jimmy Johnson (left) returned to Valley Ranch as a FOX-TV broadcaster for a reunion with Jerry Jones in 2002.

that would give us a combination of keeping our core base of players intact while also giving it something fresh, because I was being advised that they were figuring our offense out in the NFL. I feel that we did the best job of holding a team together in this time of free agency, robbing Peter to pay Paul, working the draft. It just didn't work, but we were able to hold our core base of players together over a five- or six-year period during free agency better than any NFL team's been able to do. We kept 'em. We had some unfortunate things happen [injuries] with [Charles] Haley, with Novacek, with Aikman.

"If you really want to know what in my mind tore our butts up, was that in holding this team together we had early injury-ended careers with those key guys. Haley, Novacek, Aikman, Daryl Johnston. And Deion [Sanders] with his toe injury. I probably had as good a sense on how that would affect him as anyone around, and ultimately that turned out to be the case. He went through a major reconstruction. They had to re-create his toe socket and replace ligaments. And we still don't know how that happened. We looked at when we thought it happened against Arizona in '98 a dozen times. I've been told he kicked a door at home long before the game, told it by the people who repaired the door, but I don't know that.

"Anyway, that's the route that we went down, and we bet on it, and we got bit by the earlier-ending careers of those guys. Our collective plan was that our best shot, rather than reinvent the wheel five years ago, was to keep this team together. And it wasn't a big consideration. It didn't take me all day or all week to go past that point, because I wanted to. We felt like Aikman had his skills, and we have seen healthier older players play at high levels [he offers Oakland quarterback Rich Gannon as an example], and we had retained them. We had kept them in a system [free agency] where that was really very hard to do. And we paid a price by trading out of first rounds in drafts, by letting some younger players out of here who were [salary] cap casualties.

"So that was the plan. It became very obvious to me when we lost both Aikman and[in the 2000 season opener] Galloway and wound up with that season of Aikman and [Randall] Cunningham at quarterback that we needed to start thinking differently about the future. I knew that we were going to have a tough time competing [in the spring of 2001] when Aikman left, and we had to take the $27 million hit on the cap, and we were still eating Deion's contract."

And as we talked, on the brink of the 2003 season, the similarities with what Jones had acquired in 1989 are almost startling. The team has had three losing seasons in a row, four nonwinning ones when you add the 8–8 mark in 1999. As was the case with the 1989 team, they haven't won a playoff game in six years. Again, they seem light years from glory. And in 1989 they at least had an overall first pick in the draft that would bring them Aikman. Now, as Jones says, "When we cleaned our cap up two years ago, we decided on trying to hit on a quarterback. That's why we did the [Quincy] Carter and [Chad] Hutchinson deals."

And as in 1989, when Jones never considered that what he and Johnson were doing would fail, here he sits in 2003 and says, "It has not even crossed my mind. . . . I feel as strongly, or maybe even more strongly, about the competitive get on the field, our team that can start winning ball games, as I did in 1989. Because it's the Dallas Cowboys, and because since then we have, in intermittent periods of time, done nothing but enhance the things that I bought in the Cowboys. We have lived in a period of time since then where the media and the visibility . . . we had teams that were outstanding and inter-esting with personalities and outstanding players that probably got more exposure than all the other times put together, just because of the times we live in. So if that was what motivated me in '89, to get to be a part of something with the tradition and aura and the interest, as we sit here now, football is bigger than it ever was in 1989. Bigger than it ever was before then.

"I recognize that we haven't won in the last few years. But it's just like pouring gallons of lighter fluid and letting it build up in the carpet. All we've got to do is put the match to a competitive team, and this thing will blow off the map, because it's the Dallas Cowboys."

And that's what gives Jerry Jones the chance to embark on a second rebuilding, not once more with feeling, because the feeling has already been there. This time, he's doing it once more, with Tuna.

That would be Bill ("the Tuna") Parcells, the man Jones hired to be the franchise's sixth head coach in January 2003. Parcells already has NFL Hall of Fame credentials from coaching the New York Giants and Jets and the New England Patriots. He is one of the most compelling figures in the sport, and his hiring by Jones is one of those match-to-lighter fluid situations.

"Bill is proof of where I view the future. I wouldn't have gone in the direction of Bill Parcells and made that kind of commitment had it not been to put that match to the lighter fluid. We needed to create a perception. I recognize the tangible value of perception. The last three seasons, we felt like we could hold the fort. To paraphrase Bill, if you're going to take the territory, the Super Bowl, if you do have to take a step back, don't lose the fort.

"I felt like there was a perception that had a potential to erode confidence in the decision making of the franchise, which started with me. That concerned me. We may be doing things exactly the same way we did them when we started, and we are, but the further you are removed from that success, the greater is the perception that there is a problem. Then Bill solicited this job. He told me it could be a great opportunity for all the reasons we've been talking about."

Jones had never hired a coach with NFL experience, but he also had never had a coach with the pedigree of Parcells let it be known that he'd be interested in the job if the job had an interest in him. And in working with Parcells, Jones has never been more energized. That comes in part from his experience, and in part because Parcells, he says, told him "I am fired up. I don't want to be over in the lounge show, I want to play the big room. That's where Elvis played. That's what the Cowboys are, the big room."

Bill Parcells (left) was hired by Jerry Jones as the Cowboys head coach in January 2003.

So Jones feels the old optimism. In Parcells he has a partner who challenges him. "I've never seen anyone who can approach his skills. He's just outstanding," especially at doing things the Parcells way while being sensitive to working with an owner who is also general manager. And the more sensitivity Parcells shows while applying those skills, the more Jones wants to do for his coach.

"That's what nobody has understood," he says, bubbling. "When partners are always trying to outwork each other while being sensitive, that's what makes it work. I see the same things in him that I feel. There's not a question of whether it will work."

For Jerry Jones, past is prologue. He did it before when everyone scoffed, and he's ready to do it again. Once more, with Tuna.

Without a Ring

It started because of the jerseys.

People wanted Tex Schramm to retire them. Not all of them, obviously, although there were a few years there in the early 1960s, before the Cowboys were winning anything, when some folks might have thought retiring all the jerseys and the players who wore them might not be such a bad idea.

But later, there was winning, lots of it. And in 1971 the Cowboys moved out of the Cotton Bowl into shiny new Texas Stadium in suburban Irving, and by 1975 the Cowboys had been to two of the first six Super Bowls, won one of them, been to two other conference championship games, and were establishing a legacy. A football team that does such things can do them only with some great players, and Schramm, the president and general manager and architect of it all, knew he had to find a way to memorialize the best ones.

The traditional way such things are done by teams in American professional sports is by retiring jerseys. In honor of the player who made a number great, once he retires, no one ever wears that number again. On his retirement the player is given a framed copy of that jersey, and a banner bearing the number is hung from the rafters.

Tex Schramm didn't believe in retiring jerseys.

"The way things were that first ten years," Schramm recalled, "I had a hard time figuring out who I might put in there. But when the time came, people wanted me to retire jerseys. I didn't believe in that. You retire a jersey, and you just put them away and you never really have anything from the past. I wanted something more lasting, something people would see whenever they came into the stadium and remember it."

So Schramm came up with the Ring of Honor. A player's name, uniform number and years of service would be inscribed on the stadium wall, on the ring above the main seating bowl and below the suite level. And that way, if a player came along who merited wearing the jersey of a Ring of Honor player, he could be similarly inspired whenever he came into the stadium and looked up and recalled that player.

This is what a Cowboys great's name looks like in the Ring of Honor.

(Sometimes this has worked out well. Six-time Pro Bowl linebacker Chuck Howley wore number 54 and was the fourth man inducted into the Ring of Honor, in 1977. Randy White had been given number 54 when he showed up as a rookie in 1975, and he was later inducted into the Ring himself in 1994, the same year he went into the Pro Football Hall of Fame. There's no need to mention the fellows who have worn the number since, with, uh, somewhat less success.)

Deciding who to honor with the first place in the Ring of Honor wasn't difficult. Bob Lilly was the first player ever selected by the franchise in the college draft, in the first round in 1961. He played through 1974, being selected for a franchise-record eleven Pro Bowls, being named All-Pro seven times, and earning the nickname he still holds: "Mister Cowboy." Lilly retired after the 1974 season and was inducted into the Ring of Honor on November 23, 1975.

Since then, Cowboys fans have had something else to argue about.

Parenthetically, just because the Cowboys don't officially retire numbers doesn't mean they don't do so unofficially. No one has worn 74 since Lilly retired, nor 12 since Roger Staubach hung that number up in 1979, and longtime former equipment manager Buck Buchanan once confided that was on Schramm's direction. No one has worn number 8 since Troy Aikman left after 2000, and it's a little tough to imagine Jerry Jones letting Buchanan's successor, Mike McCord, issue that number or Emmitt Smith's 22 any time soon.

But officially, the Cowboys' policy is that they don't retire jerseys. They may honor a player by trying to assign one only to newcomers considered worthy. Drew Pearson, for instance, hung up number 88 for the last time after the 1983 season, and it was five years before anyone put it on again. You might say

Michael Irvin proved himself worthy of the number. But retiring a number, no.

But the Ring of Honor is something else. Since the Cowboys started theirs in 1975, other teams have copied the idea, and usually with apparently different standards. The Buffalo Bills started what they call their Wall of Fame in 1980. The Kansas City Chiefs, who do retire numbers, have a team Hall of Fame, whose members are also commemorated Ring of Honor style on an Arrowhead Stadium wall. In Kansas City there's an annual induction, and the members are voted in by a three-person committee representing the Chiefs Booster Club, the Kansas City area media (gasp!), and the Chiefs organization.

In Dallas, the Ring of Honor is not an annual event. That tends to make it even more special, a bigger deal when there is an honoree. And the committee that does the selecting is comprised of one man. From 1975 through 1988, that was Tex Schramm. Now, it's Owner-General Manager Jerry Jones.

Even in the late 1980s, the topic of who should be in the Ring of Honor was a favorite among Cowboys fans. When Staubach was inducted in '85, he was only the sixth player so honored. By that time it was obvious that players like White and Tony Dorsett were going to merit recognition when they were done, and people started asking what that meant for all the great early era players in the interim. One such was middle linebacker Lee Roy Jordan. Popular legend held that Jordan had not been installed by Schramm because of a personal feud between the two during Jordan's playing days, but that wasn't an issue for Jones, who made Lee Roy his first Ring honoree in his first year of ownership of the team, 1989.

It was four years before there was another ceremony, for former coach Tom Landry, although that delay was Landry's doing, not Jones's. Landry had resisted the overture for several years. In 1994 Randy White and Dorsett were enshrined, in the same year they had been inducted into the Hall of Fame. (No one will say it, but Landry's recalcitrance probably kept White and Dorsett from being inducted before their Hall of Fame enshrinement, which should have been the case.)

Here and There

Of the ten players in the Cowboys' Ring of Honor, only two ever played for other NFL teams: Chuck Howley played his first two NFL seasons with the Chicago Bears, and Tony Dorsett played his last one with the Denver Broncos.

Seven more years went by before Bob Hayes, one of the franchise's greatest early stars, was inducted in 2001, just months, it turned out, before his death. Schramm, himself a Hall of Famer, will make it an even dozen posthumously in 2003.

And now three more Super Bowls have been won in the "Jones era." Now some of this era's greatest stars—Troy Aikman, Michael Irvin, Emmitt Smith—are either retired or playing elsewhere in career sunset. Now, more than ever, the debate rages. Who are the most deserving former Cowboys without a spot in the Ring of Honor? When and how should they be honored? Who should decide?

When Jones and Schramm met in March 2003 to discuss Schramm's induction, the two men reviewed, among other things, something that had become apparent: They have always shared a notion that the Ring of Honor should be an exclusive club.

Schramm said he holds the same criteria he has always held: "The Ring of Honor should be only the great players.

Not just guys who made the Pro Bowl or were popular or that kind of thing. I always felt it should be above and beyond the normal player. There's a small number who were great. They should not only be players who all the fans know, they should be the ones there is no question they have a great deal of respect for."

Independently of his conversations with Schramm, Jones long ago realized he feels the same way. Out of respect to the years of accomplishments that happened before he arrived, Jones says, "I get and listen to media input from around. I'm aware of what former players say about it, and in my mind players who played before 1989 are not eliminated from consideration, not at all. I'm battling with how to keep it exclusive but how to put in the people who ought to be up there.

"It's a battle. Where do you start? Where do you stop? [Some people say] go to Hall of Fame guys. That's the issue. How do you keep it from being a hundred people up there? And probably at some time [original franchise owner, the late] Clint [Murchison] needs to go in. It's a logistics thing."

Clearly, the one thing both Schramm and Jones wanted to avoid is a cluttering of the stadium walls that would, in their view, detract from the greatness of the contributors who are in the Ring of Honor. For what it's worth many of the team's greatest former stars disagree.

"I personally would be for a Ring of Honor that would be more inclusive," says Roger Staubach. "Jerry and Tex are both of the school to make it small and elite, and that really makes it tough. Football is a team game, and there are a lot of people that make a team. There are some guys who should be in the Ring of Honor, like Rayfield Wright and Drew Pearson, who should also be in the Hall of Fame. We had some great linemen with the Cowboys. John Niland was All-Pro for about ten years [actually Niland was a six-time Pro Bowler and a three time All-Pro]. If you look at Rayfield and Niland and Ralph Neely, we had All-Pro linemen for a long time, and those guys always take a back seat to everyone else."

Bob Lilly, it turns out, has strong feelings

A Good Omen

The Cowboys have had nine Ring of Honor ceremonies (two players being inducted together twice: Randy White and Tony Dorsett in '94, Don Meredith and Don Perkins in '76). They are 7-2 in those Ring of Honor games, losing on the days of the inductions of Lee Roy Jordan in 1989 and Bob Hayes in 2001.

on the matter, and he agrees with Staubach but takes it a step further. "I think it's too restrictive," he offers. "You can say it should be exclusive, but I would respond that's what the Hall of Fame is for. I think the Ring of Honor should be for those guys who performed over a long period, who performed consistently and well."

Not only that, but Lilly would like to see the whole process opened up. "It should be representative of every era, and I think it should be those players who should be consulted. We should be able to come up with a significant list of our teammates who played on a level to be considered. I don't know the guys who came after me as well as I do the ones I played with. I think my era, and then the Randy White era, if you want to call it that, I think those two eras have been way overlooked. There should be a committee with representatives of every era, because we know how long guys played, how well, how consistently. We know the guys who played hurt. The owners don't always know that. Cornell Green played two playoff games with ankles taped up as big as basketballs. We know that stuff. The former players should come up with a list of those to be considered, and then they could pick the Ring of Honor from that list."

Lilly's thoughts are echoed by a man who is neither in the Ring of Honor nor a candidate to be, but a man with an agenda nonetheless. Joe Avezzano was the Cowboys' special teams coach for thirteen years. In that capacity he became extremely close to one of the most popular players the Cowboys have ever had, Bill Bates, and Avezzano doesn't try to hide the fact that he's campaigning for Bates, who coached on the Cowboys' staff for five years after his retirement. This is a subject to which Avezzano has given more than a little thought, and although he applies it to one player, it's a criterion that could be more widely used.

"In my view the Ring of Honor can be reserved for highly unusual people who have made an impact on the franchise," he suggests. "When someone plays fifteen years, initiated something the NFL never had [a Pro Bowl berth for special teams coverage players, which Bates did in 1984], served the franchise for twenty years, and was one of the most popular players ever, then I think that player can merit consideration for the Ring of Honor."

Clearly he can, and perhaps he will. But Bates, who would love to be in the Ring of Honor, has said he's the first to agree there are other players who belong there first. Some of those at the top of the list are among the most vocal on the subject. All you have to do is ask, and sometimes, not even that.

By almost unanimous acclaim the two players most deserving to be part of the Ring of Honor who aren't there yet from the pre-1989 period are Rayfield Wright and Drew Pearson. Every player you talk to lists them up high. Wright, an offensive tackle who played from 1967 until 1979, was

Tackle Rayfield Wright (70) should get his place in the Ring of Honor.

selected for six Pro Bowls and was named All-Pro four times. Before Larry Allen came on the scene in 1994 and dominated in the offensive line for eight straight years, Wright was universally regarded as the best offensive lineman in team history. As many have observed, on all those great Cowboys teams of the late 60s and through the '70s, somebody had to block. The absence of Cowboys linemen from both the Ring of Honor and the Hall of Fame is ludicrous.

When Schramm talked about honoring only the greatest players in the Ring, Wright's was the first name he mentioned: "He was one of those great ones." (Only someone more cynical than I would point out that Schramm had ten years between Wright's retirement and his own departure from the team to put "the Big Cat" in the Ring.) Drew Pearson, who played with him, calls Wright "the best tackle of the '70s." Larry Cole, the big-play defensive end and tackle whose career span mirrored Wright's, says Rayfield was "the best offensive tackle I played against, even if it was in practice." The only one who won't say a whole lot about Rayfield Wright's candidacy is Rayfield Wright. He admits that it would be a big honor to be included, but like most offensive linemen, he doesn't talk about things a lot, he just goes out and does them. You get the impression from talking to Rayfield that he understands whatever impact he was going to have on the subject he had a long time ago. (Jones has noticed, too, by the way. It won't be this year, but you sense from listening to him that Rayfield Wright's inclusion in the Ring of Honor is a question of when, not if.)

On the other hand, like a lot of receivers, Drew Pearson is a little more vocal, and he's not shy about speaking up for his own candidacy.

"I do care about it," says Pearson, "because I think I deserve that recognition. I think I had that kind of career.

Drew Pearson's Hail Mary catch against the Vikings in the 1975 playoffs is one of many plays that should put him in the Ring of Honor.

When people talk about you as being a potential NFL Hall of Famer, whether you make it or not, then you must have done something to help your team. It's kind of disheartening that after you had a career like you had, you don't get that type of recognition on a team level. Then you go around the league and see other teams' rings of honor with players who haven't done half of what you've done, it's disappointing. It's frustrating. It's now been more than twenty years since I've played, though, and there's nothing you can do about it, so you just ride it out."

For what it's worth Pearson would have been right there with Wright on Schramm's list (and I'm just guessing here, but I would presume on Jones's list, as well). Said Tex of Pearson: "I'm really strong on that one. I think he should be there."

So having put it to the most unofficial of votes, we have Rayfield Wright and Drew Pearson as "musts" for the Ring of Honor. But they're not the only ones. And here's where the logistics get really interesting.

The 2005 season will be Troy Aikman's fifth year of retirement, which will make him eligible for Hall of Fame induction in 2006. Logic therefore holds that Aikman should be inducted into the Ring of Honor two seasons from now. He'll probably be the first of the post-1990 Cowboys to go in. The question then becomes, besides Wright and Pearson, do you make space for any others from pre-1989? Keep in mind, Jerry Jones has said over and over that there is no statute of limitations. You could induct Aikman in 2005 and an early era player in 2006 if you wished.

After Wright and Pearson the name most often mentioned is that of safety Cliff Harris. Cliff was a six-time Pro Bowler and four times All-Pro. "Boy, I'd love to see that," said Schramm. "He was something special and a great player." But could you induct Harris without sidekick Charlie Waters? If you subscribe to the "elite" theory, sure you could. If you're from the Lilly-Staubach school, why would you choose? Induct them both. Other names that get frequent mention from former teammates are the late Harvey Martin and tight end Billy Joe DuPree.

No one's asked for my vote, but along with Wright and Pearson, I'd cast one for Cornell Green, one of the greatest athletes in franchise history. Lilly touts his candidacy, and Green's biggest problem is that his Cowboys career ended when Bob's did, in 1974, so the number of people who saw him and can speak for him is dwindling. Cornell came in as a

Cornell Green (34) is a deserving long shot for the Ring of Honor.

raw basketball player. Lilly remembers Green's first scrimmage: "When we suited up for the first time, he had never worn hip pads, which we didn't wear in practice anyway. He put 'em on backwards, and at the end of the day his legs were all raw and bleeding. He asked some of us why we weren't having that problem, and we told him we usually wore 'em the other way around. But he overcame that. He played corner and safety. He dropped more interceptions than most players ever think of touching. If he was playing today, he could play anywhere on the field." In fourteen seasons Cornell Green played in five Pro Bowls and was named All-Pro four times, and remember, he came in when the team was two years old, before it had a pedigree. He'd make my list.

There's also the modern-day question: Who from the 1990s forward must be reserved a spot? Most of us would say Aikman, Irvin, Smith, and Larry Allen for sure, and the case is building for safety Darren Woodson.

So the question remains, where do you draw the line without diminishing the Ring of Honor's impact? Drew Pearson says, "You draw the line when you run out of players who deserve that recognition. Don't let a number dictate what goes up there. If they're a significant part of Cowboy history, they deserve that recognition. There shouldn't be a set number. It should be what they meant to this organization."

And if you're a Cowboys fan, you see the problem Jerry Jones has inherited. Because to the Cowboys, they're all special. But there is a consensus: Rayfield and Drew need a spot in the Ring.

About the Author

Brad Sham is a native of Chicago, a graduate of the University of Missouri's School of Journalism, and a thirty-three-year resident of Dallas, which makes him a naturalized Texan. In addition to broadcasting Cowboys games for twenty-five years, he has called Dallas Burn games in Major League Soccer for six years, and has also broadcast fifteen Cotton Bowl Classics and numerous NFL and NCAA football and basketball games for CBS Radio/Westwood One. A former radio and television broadcaster for baseball's Texas Rangers, he proves his basic human optimism by being a lifelong Chicago Cubs fan.

Sham has been named Texas Sportscaster of the Year eight times, has won seven Katie Awards from the Press Club of Dallas, and in 2002 was a member of the inaugural class of the Texas Radio Hall of Fame. He lives with his wife, son, and two spoiled dogs in the Dallas suburb of Coppell.